Conte[nts]

◀ **Use What You Know** ▶

 Adding and Subtracting: Using Facts

 Place Value: Developing Number Sense

 Adding and Subtracting: 2-Digit Numbers

Adding and Subtracting

Time and Money

Understanding Multiplication

Multiplication: Using Facts

8 Understanding Division

9 Division: Using Facts

10 Geometry

11 Measurement

Fractions and Decimals

 Multiplying and Dividing by 1-Digit Numbers

Addition
Counting On and Make a Ten

Find the sum.

| 1. $\begin{array}{r} 3 \\ +5 \\ \hline \end{array}$ | 2. $\begin{array}{r} 7 \\ +4 \\ \hline \end{array}$ | 3. $\begin{array}{r} 6 \\ +5 \\ \hline \end{array}$ | 4. $\begin{array}{r} 8 \\ +4 \\ \hline \end{array}$ | 5. $\begin{array}{r} 9 \\ +6 \\ \hline \end{array}$ | 6. $\begin{array}{r} 8 \\ +3 \\ \hline \end{array}$ | 7. $\begin{array}{r} 5 \\ +8 \\ \hline \end{array}$ |

| 8. $\begin{array}{r} 7 \\ +7 \\ \hline \end{array}$ | 9. $\begin{array}{r} 6 \\ +7 \\ \hline \end{array}$ | 10. $\begin{array}{r} 9 \\ +2 \\ \hline \end{array}$ | 11. $\begin{array}{r} 9 \\ +3 \\ \hline \end{array}$ | 12. $\begin{array}{r} 8 \\ +2 \\ \hline \end{array}$ | 13. $\begin{array}{r} 7 \\ +5 \\ \hline \end{array}$ | 14. $\begin{array}{r} 6 \\ +6 \\ \hline \end{array}$ |

15. $3 + 6 = $ ___   16. $2 + 9 = $ ___   17. $8 + 8 = $ ___

18. $5 + 5 = $ ___   19. $8 + 7 = $ ___   20. $4 + 6 = $ ___

Mixed Applications

Solve. Label your answer.

21. Ben had 8 fish in his aquarium. He bought 7 more fish. How many fish does Ben have in his aquarium now?

_____

22. Meg sees 5 rainbow fish at the aquarium, but 3 other rainbow fish are hidden. How many rainbow fish are there?

_____

| VISUAL THINKING |

This number line shows $3 + 5 = 8$.

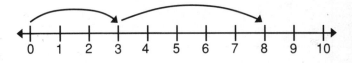

Match each addition sentence to a number line.

23. $4 + 5 = 9$

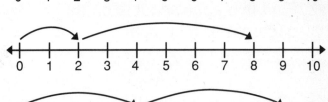

24. $6 + 4 = 10$

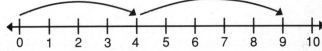

25. $2 + 6 = 8$

Addition
Doubles and Doubles Plus One

Find the sum.

1. $\begin{array}{r}3\\+3\\\hline\end{array}$	2. $\begin{array}{r}7\\+8\\\hline\end{array}$	3. $\begin{array}{r}6\\+9\\\hline\end{array}$	4. $\begin{array}{r}8\\+5\\\hline\end{array}$	5. $\begin{array}{r}9\\+8\\\hline\end{array}$	6. $\begin{array}{r}2\\+3\\\hline\end{array}$	7. $\begin{array}{r}5\\+4\\\hline\end{array}$
8. $\begin{array}{r}5\\+5\\\hline\end{array}$	9. $\begin{array}{r}6\\+7\\\hline\end{array}$	10. $\begin{array}{r}3\\+8\\\hline\end{array}$	11. $\begin{array}{r}2\\+2\\\hline\end{array}$	12. $\begin{array}{r}8\\+7\\\hline\end{array}$	13. $\begin{array}{r}4\\+7\\\hline\end{array}$	14. $\begin{array}{r}6\\+6\\\hline\end{array}$

15. $5 + 8 =$ ___   16. $6 + 5 =$ ___   17. $4 + 4 =$ ___

18. $8 + 9 =$ ___   19. $5 + 9 =$ ___   20. $7 + 7 =$ ___

21. $9 + 7 =$ ___   22. $7 + 6 =$ ___   23. $9 + 9 =$ ___

24. $8 + 8 =$ ___   25. $4 + 5 =$ ___   26. $8 + 6 =$ ___

27. $5 + 5 =$ ___   28. $6 + 6 =$ ___   29. $7 + 8 =$ ___

Mixed Applications

30. Kate bought a 6-ounce box of dog treats. A large box is double the weight of the 6-ounce box. How much does a large box weigh?

_____

31. Kate got her dog when he was 7 months old. That was 3 months ago. How old is Kate's dog now?

_____

NUMBER SENSE

32. Find five *doubles* facts on this page. Write their sums.

33. Find five *doubles plus one* facts. Write their sums.

___ ___ ___ ___ ___   ___ ___ ___ ___ ___

Mental Math:
Order and Zero

Find the sum.

1. $5 + 0 =$ ___

2. $0 + 6 =$ ___

3. $4 + 4 =$ ___

4. $8 + 8 =$ ___

5. $9 + 0 =$ ___

6. $0 + 7 =$ ___

7. $\begin{array}{r} 5 \\ +7 \\ \hline \end{array}$ $\begin{array}{r} 7 \\ +5 \\ \hline \end{array}$

8. $\begin{array}{r} 6 \\ +8 \\ \hline \end{array}$ $\begin{array}{r} 8 \\ +6 \\ \hline \end{array}$

9. $\begin{array}{r} 3 \\ +9 \\ \hline \end{array}$ $\begin{array}{r} 9 \\ +3 \\ \hline \end{array}$

Use order in addition to write another addition fact.

10. $8 + 7 = 15$, so ___ $+$ ___ $=$ ___

11. $9 + 4 = 13$, so ___ $+$ ___ $=$ ___

Mixed Applications

12. Lillian threw fish to two penguins. All the fish were caught. One penguin caught 7 fish. The other penguin caught no fish. How many fish did Lillian throw?

_____

13. The penguins perch on rocks. There are 5 penguins on the small rock. There are twice as many on the large rock. How many penguins are on the large rock?

_____

| **WRITER'S CORNER** |

14. Write a word problem for the picture. Exchange with a partner. Solve.

_____

_____

_____

_____

Name _____

Addition
Grouping Addends

Look for tens. Find the sum.

1. $5 + 5 + 2 =$ ___

2. $4 + 2 + 8 =$ ___

3. $6 + 1 + 5 =$ ___

4. $3 + 7 + 8 =$ ___

5. $2 + 4 + 6 =$ ___

6. $9 + 1 + 1 =$ ___

7. $3 + 2 + 8 =$ ___

8. $7 + 2 + 2 =$ ___

9. $5 + 5 + 5 =$ ___

10.	11.	12.	13.	14.	15.	16.
5	8	4	7	6	9	3
4	1	6	5	4	0	3
+6	+9	+3	+5	+7	+4	+7

17.	18.	19.	20.	21.	22.	23.
9	8	2	1	7	6	5
1	6	8	4	3	5	8
+7	+4	+5	+6	+8	+4	+2

Mixed Applications

24. There were 6 robins in a nest. Then 2 more robins flew in. How many robins are there now?

_____

25. Mrs. Goody has 6 dogs, 4 horses, and 3 cats. How many pets does Mrs. Goody have?

_____

VISUAL THINKING

26. Ring the dogs below to make three groups. Write an addition sentence that tells what you did.

___ + ___ + ___ = ___   Did you find a ten? _____

Use with text pages 8–9.

Name _____

Problem-Solving Strategy
Act It Out

Act it out or use objects to solve.

1. During Animal Activity Day, the animals lined up from tallest to shortest. Pablo Pony is taller than Perry Penguin. Herman Hamster is shorter than Perry Penguin. Gary Giraffe is taller than Pablo Pony. How were the animals lined up?

_____

_____

2. Four animals ran in the big race. The cheetah beat the horse. The dog came in after the cat. The horse beat the dog and the cat. In what order did the animals finish?

_____

_____

Mixed Applications

3. The Berg family is eighth in a line of 12 families waiting to see the Animal Film Festival. Are there more families in front of the Bergs or behind them?

_____

4. Darcy's dog show stars 5 poodles, 3 beagles, and 7 spaniels. How many dogs appear in the show?

_____

WRITER'S CORNER

5. Write a word problem about the picture below. Use one of the problems above to get ideas.

_____
_____
_____
_____
_____

Subtraction
Counting Back and Counting Up

Find the difference.

1. 8
   −5
   ___

2. 7
   −3
   ___

3. 6
   −2
   ___

4. 10
   − 3
   ___

5. 9
   −7
   ___

6. 8
   −1
   ___

7. 5
   −4
   ___

8. 7
   −4
   ___

9. 6
   −3
   ___

10. 9
    −6
    ___

11. 9
    −4
    ___

12. 8
    −7
    ___

13. 7
    −6
    ___

14. 6
    −1
    ___

15. 7 − 5 = ___

16. 10 − 8 = ___

17. 8 − 1 = ___

18. 9 − 4 = ___

19. 6 − 4 = ___

20. 10 − 9 = ___

Mixed Applications

21. Al's cat had 7 kittens. He gave away all of the kittens but 2. How many kittens did Al give away?

_____

22. Rosa bought 6 cans of turkey dinner and 3 cans of liver lunch for her kittens. How many more cans of turkey did Rosa buy?

_____

| **EVERYDAY MATH CONNECTION** |

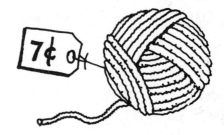

23. The pet store is having a sale on all cat toys. Every item is 3¢ off the marked price. Find the sale price of each item.

   rattle ___   catnip mouse ___   yarn ball ___

Subtraction
Sames and Zeros

Find the difference.

1. 8 −8	**2.** 12 − 3	**3.** 15 − 7	**4.** 10 − 0	**5.** 9 −6	**6.** 11 − 5	**7.** 5 −5
8. 10 − 5	**9.** 6 −5	**10.** 9 −0	**11.** 13 − 4	**12.** 9 −9	**13.** 13 − 6	**14.** 6 −0
15. 15 − 7	**16.** 7 −7	**17.** 6 −6	**18.** 5 −0	**19.** 10 − 10	**20.** 12 − 4	**21.** 9 −8

22. $14 - 9 =$ ___   **23.** $8 - 0 =$ ___   **24.** $4 - 4 =$ ___

25. $5 - 0 =$ ___   **26.** $3 - 3 =$ ___   **27.** $7 - 0 =$ ___

Mixed Applications

28. Jo's cat had 5 kittens. Jo gave all of the kittens away on Saturday. How many kittens did Jo have left on Sunday?

_____

29. The pet hotel keeps dogs and cats. They are keeping no dogs and 9 cats. How many pets is the pet hotel keeping now?

_____

LOGICAL REASONING

Complete each number sentence. Write + or − in the ◯.

30. 13 ◯ 6 = 7   **31.** 2 ◯ 2 = 0   **32.** 4 ◯ 4 = 8

33. 10 ◯ 1 = 9   **34.** 8 ◯ 8 = 16   **35.** 9 ◯ 7 = 16

36. 14 ◯ 7 = 7   **37.** 9 ◯ 1 = 10   **38.** 10 ◯ 10 = 0

Connecting Addition and Subtraction

Write a related subtraction fact.

1. 7 + 8 = 15, so ___ – ___ = ___   2. 9 + 6 = 15, so ___ – ___ = ___

3. 9 + 3 = 12, so ___ – ___ = ___   4. 8 + 9 = 17, so ___ – ___ = ___

5. 6 + 5 = 11, so ___ – ___ = ___   6. 7 + 7 = 14, so ___ – ___ = ___

Write a related addition fact.

7. 16 – 8 = 8, so ___ + ___ = ___   8. 13 – 6 = 7, so ___ + ___ = ___

9. 15 – 9 = 6, so ___ + ___ = ___   10. 12 – 4 = 8, so ___ + ___ = ___

11. 11 – 8 = 3, so ___ + ___ = ___   12. 14 – 5 = 9, so ___ + ___ = ___

Mixed Applications

13. There are 7 spider monkeys and 8 woolly monkeys in the large cage. How many monkeys are in the cage?

_____

14. Each large monkey eats 8 bananas at lunchtime. Each small monkey eats only 4 bananas. How many more bananas does each large monkey eat?

_____

VISUAL THINKING

15. Write an addition sentence and a subtraction sentence that tell about the picture below.

___ + ___ = ___   ___ – ___ = ___

Mental Math:
Fact Families

Write the set of numbers for each fact family.

1. $4 + 8 = 12$; $8 + 4 = 12$; $12 - 4 = 8$; $12 - 8 = 4$ _____

2. $6 + 7 = 13$; $7 + 6 = 13$; $13 - 7 = 6$; $13 - 6 = 7$ _____

Write the fact family for each set of numbers.

3. 7, 8, 15

___ + ___ = ___

___ + ___ = ___

___ - ___ = ___

___ - ___ = ___

4. 9, 4, 13

___ + ___ = ___

___ + ___ = ___

___ - ___ = ___

___ - ___ = ___

5. 6, 8, 14

___ + ___ = ___

___ + ___ = ___

___ - ___ = ___

___ - ___ = ___

Find the missing number to complete each fact.

6. $9 + $ ___ $ = 15$ $6 + $ ___ $ = 15$ $15 - $ ___ $ = 9$ $15 - $ ___ $ = 6$

Mixed Applications

7. Ethan had 7 jungle animal stickers. He got 8 more. Write a number sentence to tell how many he has now.

_____

8. Write the three other facts in the same fact family.

_____

_____

_____

VISUAL THINKING

9. What two facts describe this domino?

___ + ___ = ___ ; ___ - ___ = ___

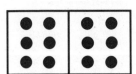

10. Why are there only two facts?

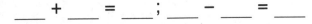

Addition and Subtraction
Missing Addends

Find the missing addend.

1. $5 + \underline{\quad} = 12$

2. $3 + \underline{\quad} = 12$

3. $\underline{\quad} + 7 = 13$

4. $8 + \underline{\quad} = 16$

5. $\underline{\quad} + 6 = 15$

6. $8 + \underline{\quad} = 17$

7. $\underline{\quad} + 9 = 13$

8. $\underline{\quad} + 7 = 12$

9. $5 + \underline{\quad} = 14$

10. $\underline{\quad} + 6 = 12$

11. $9 + \underline{\quad} = 12$

12. $\underline{\quad} + 6 = 14$

13. $\underline{\quad} + 8 = 15$

14. $\underline{\quad} + 7 = 14$

15. $9 + \underline{\quad} = 18$

16. $4 + \underline{\quad} = 12$

17. $\underline{\quad} + 9 = 11$

18. $5 + \underline{\quad} = 11$

Mixed Applications

19. Howard Husky, a race dog, runs 6 miles the first day of training. His total after two days is 11 miles. How many miles does Howard run the second day?

_____

20. Ms. Butcher has 8 dogs on her racing team when training season begins. By the end of the season, she has 15 dogs. How many dogs does she add to her team?

_____

MIXED REVIEW

Find the sum or difference.

1. $\begin{array}{r} 8 \\ +5 \\ \hline \end{array}$

2. $\begin{array}{r} 5 \\ +9 \\ \hline \end{array}$

3. $\begin{array}{r} 13 \\ -7 \\ \hline \end{array}$

4. $\begin{array}{r} 16 \\ -8 \\ \hline \end{array}$

5. $\begin{array}{r} 9 \\ -9 \\ \hline \end{array}$

6. $\begin{array}{r} 7 \\ +7 \\ \hline \end{array}$

7. $9 + 9 = \underline{\quad}$

8. $15 - 7 = \underline{\quad}$

9. $12 - 4 = \underline{\quad}$

Use with text pages 22–23.

Choosing
Addition or Subtraction

Complete each number sentence.

Write + or − in the ◯.

1. 5 ◯ 9 = 14

2. 8 ◯ 3 = 5

3. 15 ◯ 6 = 9

4. 12 ◯ 7 = 5

5. 7 ◯ 4 = 11

6. 3 ◯ 8 = 1

7. 13 ◯ 6 = 7

8. 9 ◯ 8 = 1

9. 14 ◯ 7 =

10. 9 ◯ 8 = 17

11. 7 ◯ 6 = 13

12. 12 ◯ 4 =

13. 13 ◯ 8 = 5

14. 9 ◯ 6 = 3

15. 3 ◯ 9 = 12

Mixed Applications

16. Sport ate 5 puppy treats out of the new box. The box had 14 treats when it was opened. How many treats are left in the box?

_____

17. Ling got her puppy, Rex, when it was 8 weeks old. Rex is 17 weeks old now. For how many weeks has Ling had Rex?

_____

WRITER'S CORNER

18. Write an addition word problem and a subtraction word problem. Use the picture for ideas. Write the number sentence that you would use to solve each problem.

_____

_____

_____

____ + ____ = ____

_____

_____

_____

____ − ____ = ____

Problem Solving
Choose a Strategy

| Mixed Applications ⟩ | STRATEGIES | • Act It Out   • Guess and Check   • Make a Model
• Draw a Picture   • Write a Number Sentence |

Choose a strategy and solve.

1. Cathy and Juanita have 14 gerbils. Cathy has 2 more gerbils than Juanita. How many gerbils does each girl have?

   _____

   _____

2. Ed walks his dog 15 minutes every day. He walks 3 minutes less at noon than after dinner. For how many minutes does Ed walk his dog at each time?

   _____

   _____

3. Hank spent $16 at the book sale. He spent $2 less on the fish book than he spent on the bird magazine. How much did Hank spend on each item?

   _____

   _____

4. Marta has a total of 17 goldfish in her tank. She has 5 more lionhead fish than fantail fish. How many of each kind of goldfish does Marta have?

   _____

   _____

5. Four children are standing in line. Matt is behind Pedro and in front of Bill. Sally is in front of Pedro. Who is first in line? Who is last?

   _____

   _____

6. Dan has 15 animals on his farm. He has 5 cows and 3 goats. The rest of the animals are chickens. How many chickens does Dan have on his farm?

   _____

   _____

NUMBER SENSE

7. Look again at Exercises 1 and 2. What did you do if your first guess was not correct?

   _____

   _____

Number Patterns

Tell whether each number is *odd* or *even*.

1. 62 _____   2. 29 _____   3. 17 _____

4. 140 _____   5. 243 _____   6. 456 _____

Write the missing numbers in the pattern.

7. 10, _____, 30, 40, _____, _____, 70

8. 35, 30, _____, 20, _____, _____, 5

9. 23, 25, 27, _____, _____, 33, _____

10. Sharon is counting baseball cards by twos. She counts 22, 24, 26, 28. What numbers come before 22 and after 28? ____, 22, 24, 26, 28, ____

Mixed Applications

11. Dan noticed a pattern at his school. The classroom doors are numbered with every other odd number. They begin at 21 and end at 49. Write the numbers.

____ ____ ____ ____

____ ____ ____ ____

12. Gigi likes to count by twos, but she sometimes makes mistakes. Mark an X through the numbers that do not belong in Gigi's pattern.

28, 29, 30, 32, 34,

35, 36, 37, 38, 40

NUMBER SENSE

13. Look at the numbers for Exercises 1–13 on this page. Ring the odd numbers in red and the even numbers in blue. If there were a 14th problem, what color would the ring be? Why?

_____

_____

Numbers to Hundreds

Write the number.

1. 700 + 20 + 3 = _____

2. 100 + 0 + 9 = _____

3. 400 + 70 + 5 = _____

4. 300 + 10 + 6 = _____

5. five hundred seventy-nine _____

6. seven hundred forty _____

7. 4 hundreds 8 tens 5 ones _____

8. 6 hundreds 1 ten 0 ones _____

Complete the table. Write the number that is 100
less. Write the number that is 100 more.

	100 Less	Number	100 More
9.	_____	134	_____
10.	_____	456	_____
11.	_____	872	_____
12.	_____	507	_____

Mixed Applications

Choose the best answer. Write the number on
the blank.

13. Julie, a third-grade student, is
    about ____ feet tall.

    4   40   400

14. There are about ____ students on
    Rockville School's soccer team.

    15   150   1,500

EVERYDAY MATH CONNECTION

Kelsey is writing a news story for the school paper
about the school cafeteria. The food service manager
tells him that six hundred eighty-three salads and
nine hundred forty-seven containers of milk are served
each day. What numbers should Kelsey write down?

15. _____ salads

16. _____ containers of milk

Name _____

Comparing Numbers

Compare the numbers. Write <, >, or = in the ◯.

1.

Tens	Ones
2	3
3	1

23 ◯ 31

2.

Tens	Ones
5	0
4	9

50 ◯ 49

3.

Hundreds	Tens	Ones
2	8	0
2	0	8

280 ◯ 208

4.

Tens	Ones
8	5
8	5

85 ◯ 85

5.

Tens	Ones
7	9
9	0

79 ◯ 90

6.

Hundreds	Tens	Ones
4	8	5
4	8	4

485 ◯ 484

7. 7 ◯ 9

8. 47 ◯ 42

9. 85 ◯ 79

10. 91 ◯ 91

11. 467 ◯ 567

12. 2 ◯ 256

13. 921 ◯ 920

14. 860 ◯ 890

15. Write 93 > 88 in words.

_____

Mixed Applications

16. Micki drove 46 miles to the museum, and Vicki drove 51 miles. Who traveled farther?

_____

17. Ezra spent $5.50 on a taxi ride to the city. Bud's bus ride to the city cost $4.95. Who spent less?

_____

VISUAL THINKING

Use the map to answer these questions.

18. Is San Francisco closer to Seattle or to Salt Lake City?

_____

19. Is Los Angeles closer to San Francisco or to Salt Lake City?

Seattle
808 mi
Salt Lake City
636 mi
San Francisco
379 mi
715 mi
Los Angeles

Ordering Numbers

Write the numbers in order from least to greatest.

1. 83, 87, 80

2. 38, 31, 35

3. 92, 96, 94

_____

_____

_____

4. 246, 251, 297

5. 897, 803, 830

6. 550, 505, 555

_____

_____

_____

Write the numbers in order from greatest to least.

7. 337, 373, 341

8. 689, 698, 675

9. 762, 726, 750

_____

_____

_____

10. 501, 510, 515

11. 432, 423, 430

12. 907, 970, 957

_____

_____

_____

Mixed Applications

13. Gil collected 17 shells on Sunday and 15 shells on Monday. Did he collect more or less than 30 shells?

_____

14. A plane traveled 557 miles south and 657 miles east. In which direction did it travel farther? How many miles farther?

_____

MIXED REVIEW

Find the sum or difference.

1. $\begin{array}{r} 8 \\ +5 \\ \hline \end{array}$

2. $\begin{array}{r} 7 \\ +8 \\ \hline \end{array}$

3. $\begin{array}{r} 9 \\ -3 \\ \hline \end{array}$

4. $\begin{array}{r} 12 \\ -\ 4 \\ \hline \end{array}$

5. $\begin{array}{r} 5 \\ +9 \\ \hline \end{array}$

6. $\begin{array}{r} 17 \\ -\ 8 \\ \hline \end{array}$

Find the missing addend.

7. $7 + \underline{} = 13$

8. $8 + \underline{} = 14$

9. $\underline{} + 5 = 12$

Exploring Estimation
Rounding

Round to the nearest ten cents or the nearest ten.

1. 43 _____

2. 79 _____

3. 89 _____

4. 61 _____

5. 33¢ _____

6. 47¢ _____

7. 62¢ _____

8. 85¢ _____

9. 54 _____

10. 58¢ _____

11. 19 _____

12. 45¢ _____

Write the numbers in each row that round to the number in the box.

13. 85 83 78 75 73 88 $\boxed{80}$ _____

14. 63¢ 71¢ 65¢ 67¢ 69¢ $\boxed{70¢}$ _____

15. Write the numbers that round to 10.

_____

16. Kathy estimates that she saw about 50 geese at the pond. What is the least number of geese she may have seen? the greatest number?

_____

17. Kathy's suitcase weighs between 20 and 30 pounds, but she thinks it weighs closer to 20 pounds. What could the weight of her suitcase be?

_____

CONSUMER CONNECTION

18. You are told that you can spend "about 50¢" at the toy store. Which items can you choose from?

_____

Estimation
Rounding to the Nearest Hundred

Use the number line. Round each number to the
nearest hundred.

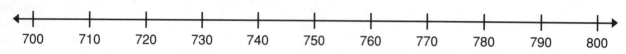

700	710	720	730	740	750	760	770	780	790	800

1. 785 _____   2. 742 _____   3. 719 _____   4. 752 _____

Round each number to the nearest hundred.

5. 587 _____   6. 279 _____   7. 848 _____   8. 920 _____

9. 328 _____   10. 489 _____   11. 176 _____   12. 512 _____

Write the number that is halfway between the
two hundreds.

13. 300, 400 _____   14. 800, 900 _____   15. 600, 700 _____

Mixed Applications

16. A jet crew is made up of 2
pilots, 8 flight attendants, and 1
flight supervisor. How many
people are in the crew?

_____

17. The small jet carried 378
people from New York to
Washington. To the nearest
hundred, about how many
people were on the flight?

_____

NUMBER SENSE ─────────────────────────

18. Does rounding to the nearest ten
or rounding to the nearest hundred
give a closer estimate? Explain.

Example
378
to the nearest ten—380
to the nearest hundred—400

_____
_____
_____
_____

Use with text pages 46–47.

Name _____

USE WHAT YOU KNOW

Problem Solving
Use a Table

The Social Studies teacher at Kaplan School took a survey to find out what field trip his students wanted to take. He made a table to show the most popular choices and the number of votes for each.

Students' Votes for Field Trip	
Field Trip Ideas	Votes
City Hall	55
Fire Station	87
Electric Company	23
Police Station	119

1. Which field trip idea got the greatest number of votes?

2. Which idea got closest to 100 votes?

Mixed Applications → **STRATEGIES** • Guess and Check • Act It Out • Use a Table

3. There were more votes for the Courthouse than for the Civic Center, and more for the Animal Shelter than for the Courthouse. Which of these ideas got the fewest votes?

4. Out of 10 field trip ideas, the Art Museum was the sixth most popular. How many field trip ideas were more popular than the Art Museum?

SOCIAL STUDIES CONNECTION

5. Ask ten students in your class to vote for visiting City Hall, the Fire Station, the Electric Company, or the Police Station. Show your results in the table.

6. Which trip idea received the most votes? the fewest?

Students' Votes for Field Trip	
Field Trip Ideas	Votes
City Hall	
Fire Station	
Electric Company	
Police Station	

Use with text pages 48–49.

HBJ material copyrighted under notice appearing earlier in this work.

Exploring Place Value

Write each number in standard form in the place-value chart.

Thousands	Hundreds	Tens	Ones

1. eighty-seven

2. four hundred thirty-two

3. nine hundred five

4. four thousand, seven hundred seven

5. six thousand, twenty-four

6. seven thousand, one hundred forty-five

7. two thousand, one

Mixed Applications

8. Mr. Taylor gets a check for one thousand, four hundred twenty-seven dollars. How would the amount be written in standard form?

_____

9. Sue earns eight hundred forty-three dollars a week. Ken earns seven hundred eighty-nine dollars a week. Who earns more?

_____

10. Ms. Huang's monthly pay is $2,045. This month, she is given an extra $1,000 bonus. What is her pay this month?

_____

LOGICAL REASONING

Choose the best answer. Write **a, b, c,** or **d.**

11. There are about ____ pages in your math book.

   a. 4   **b.** 40   **c.** 400   **d.** 4,000

Use with text pages 52–53.

Comparing and Ordering to Ten Thousands

Compare the numbers. Write <, >, or = in the ◯.

1. 5,809 ◯ 4,908

2. 9,042 ◯ 8,998

3. 2,468 ◯ 1,357

4. 23,412 ◯ 19,246

5. 18,590 ◯ 18,650

6. 45,847 ◯ 45,847

Write the numbers in order from least to greatest.

7. 2,345
    22,486
    12,123

8. 32,076
    32,570
    23,676

9. 70,291
    68,921
    69,129

10. 99,909
    99,900
    99,099

_____ _____ _____ _____

_____ _____ _____ _____

_____ _____ _____ _____

Mixed Applications

11. Map A shows an area of 12,000 square miles. Map B shows 11,979 square miles. Which map shows a greater area?

_____

12. The area of Montana is one hundred forty-seven thousand, forty-six square miles. Write the area in numbers.

_____

| SOCIAL STUDIES CONNECTION |

13. Use the table to order the areas of the Great Lakes from greatest to least.

_____

_____

_____

_____

_____

Areas of the Great Lakes

Name	Area (in square miles)
Huron	23,000
Superior	31,700
Erie	9,910
Michigan	22,300
Ontario	7,550

Numbers to Hundred Thousands

Write the value of the digit 5 in each number.

1. 12,500 _____

2. 325,443 _____

3. 753,219 _____

4. 543,210 _____

Write each number in standard form.

5. 200,000 + 30,000 + 2,000 + 70 + 4 _____

6. seventy thousand, eight hundred twenty _____

Complete the table. Use a calculator to find the numbers that are 1,000 more, 10,000 more, and 100,000 more.

	Number	1,000 More	10,000 More	100,000 More
7.	31,096			
8.	249,861			
9.	890,421			
10.	621,940			

Mixed Applications

11. On Sunday, 375,000 people visited state parks. By three o'clock, 100,000 people had gone home. How many people were still at the parks?

_____

12. Ana picked 5 red apples and 10 green apples. Hoa picked 9 apples of each color. Who picked more apples? How many more?

_____

NUMBER SENSE _____

13. Find and write the greatest number on this page. _____

Name _____

Ordinal Numbers

Use the pattern 0, 5, 10, 15, 20, 25, 30, . . . for Exercises 1–2.

1. What is the fifth number in this pattern? _____

2. What will be the eighth number in this pattern? _____

The table shows the order of the letters of the alphabet. Use the table for Exercises 3–6.

A	B	C	D	E	F	G	H	I	J	K	L	M	N	O	P	Q	R	S	T	U	V	W	X	Y	Z
1	2	3	4	5	6	7	8	9	10	11	12	13	14	15	16	17	18	19	20	21	22	23	24	25	26

3. What is the fourth letter?

_____

4. What is the seventh letter?

_____

5. What is the twelfth letter?

_____

6. The letter **M** is in which place?

_____

Mixed Applications

7. The letter **K** is eleventh in the alphabet. How many letters come before it?

_____

8. When the states are listed in alphabetical order, the list begins like this: Alabama, Alaska, Arizona, Arkansas, Connecticut, . . . In what place is Connecticut?

_____

LANGUAGE ARTS CONNECTION

You can write an ordinal number in word form, or you can write a short form by writing the last two letters of the word form after the number.

eighth

8th

In each pair of ordinal numbers, ring the two letters that are the same.

9. sixty-second   62nd

10. twenty-first   21st

11. third   3rd

Problem-Solving Strategy
Make a Table

This list shows attendance at RFK Stadium for eight weeks.

Week 1	33,916	Week 5	28,246
Week 2	21,907	Week 6	19,886
Week 3	14,592	Week 7	31,991
Week 4	21,234	Week 8	44,045

1. Make a table. Order the attendance figures from least to greatest.

2. In which week was attendance greatest? _____

3. In which week were the fewest people present? _____

4. In which weeks was attendance over 30,000? _____

Mixed Applications ▷ | **STRATEGIES** | • Guess and Check • Make a Table • Act It Out

5. Maria sells more hot dogs than Sam and fewer than Ana. Ben sells fewer hot dogs than Sam. Who sells the most hot dogs?

_____

6. Seth buys a large drink for $2.25. A bag of popcorn makes the total $1.00 more. What is Seth's total?

_____

VISUAL THINKING

7. Write the number in standard form.

_____

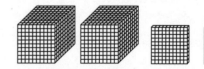

8. What number is 1,000 more?

_____

9. What number is 100 less?

_____

Use with text pages 60–61.

Estimating Sums and Differences

Estimate each sum or difference by rounding.
Show your work.

1. 48 _____
    + 19 + _____
         _____

2. 21 _____
    + 67 + _____
         _____

3. 87 _____
    − 41 − _____
         _____

4. 89 _____
    + 53 + _____
         _____

5. 70 _____
    − 27 − _____
         _____

6. 62 _____
    + 98 + _____
         _____

7. 39 _____
    + 72 + _____
         _____

8. 57 _____
    − 18 − _____
         _____

Mixed Applications

9. There are 58 reptiles inside the Reptile House and 19 reptiles outside. To the nearest ten, how many reptiles are there in all?

_____

10. The Mane Shop at the zoo sold 48 lion posters and 72 panda posters. To the nearest ten, how many more panda posters did they sell?

_____

MIXED REVIEW

Write the standard form.

1. 30,000 + 8,000 + 400 + 70 + 1

_____

2. 400,000 + 6,000 + 900 + 30 + 5

_____

3. 50,000 + 4,000 + 700 + 20 + 3

_____

4. 700,000 + 30,000 + 400 + 3

_____

Write the numbers in order from least to greatest.

5. 1,900; 1,759; 2,030

_____

6. 4,657; 4,115; 3,898

_____

Name _____

Adding One- and Two-Digit Numbers

Estimate the sum by rounding.

1. 42 +37	2. 86 + 8	3. 39 +56	4. 21 +69	5. 68 +12	6. 19 +23

7. 61 + 3	8. 22 + 9	9. 37 +21	10. 42 +11	11. 16 +68	12. 27 +33

Find the sum.

13. 62 +15	14. 79 + 2	15. 28 +47	16. 35 +38	17. 23 + 9	18. 41 +28

19. 69 +21	20. 52 +29	21. 63 +28	22. 49 +49	23. 82 + 9	24. 68 +12

Mixed Applications

25. It takes 38 minutes in the morning and 42 minutes in the evening to feed the seals. To the nearest ten, how many minutes does feeding the seals take?

_____

26. The monkeys snack on 18 bananas and 9 apples each afternoon. How many pieces of fruit do the monkeys eat in all?

_____

EVERYDAY MATH CONNECTION

27. Marielle buys two small bags of peanuts for $0.35 each. George buys one large bag for $0.75. Who spends more money? How much more?

_____

Use with text pages 72–73.

Adding Two-Digit Numbers

Estimate the sum by rounding.

1.	39 + 47	2.	76 + 19	3.	58 + 39	4.	90 + 11	5.	76 + 41	6.	48 + 87

Find the sum.

7.	78 + 27	8.	55 + 96	9.	9 + 97	10.	88 + 34	11.	29 + 78	12.	43 + 76
13.	81 + 33	14.	67 + 58	15.	91 + 43	16.	41 + 37	17.	29 + 98	18.	57 + 89
19.	43 + 77	20.	32 + 46	21.	48 + 97	22.	32 + 26	23.	39 + 87	24.	13 + 52

Mixed Applications

25. The dolphin show is 27 minutes long. The seal show lasts 25 minutes. How long are both shows combined?

_____

26. The animal trainer feeds the porpoises two buckets of fish. Each bucket contains 87 fish. How many fish do they eat in all?

_____

LOGICAL REASONING

27. Two addends combine to make a sum of about 80. One addend is 56. Is the other addend less than or greater than 56?

_____

28. Three addends combine to make a sum of about 100. Two of the addends are less than 20. Is the third addend less than or greater than 50?

_____

Adding More Than Two Addends

Estimate the sum. Show your work.

1. 23 ____	2. 46 ____	3. 78 ____	4. 27 ____
19 ____	18 ____	21 ____	39 ____
+43 + ____	+31 + ____	+32 + ____	+42 + ____
____	____	____	____

Find the sum.

5. 87	6. 71	7. 22	8. 54	9. 65	10. 51
32	39	46	19	59	28
+19	+42	+38	+68	+11	+28

11. 43 + 35 + 19 = ____

12. 46 + 28 + 37 = ____

Mixed Applications

13. The circus performs a total of 4 shows more during the week than on the weekend. If there are 2 shows each weekday, how many shows are there in a weekend? in a week?

_____

14. The circus show has 17 dogs, 19 horses, and 12 tigers. How many dogs, horses, and tigers are there in the show?

_____

NUMBER SENSE

Find the sum.

15. 25 + 99 = _____

16. 35 + 99 = _____

17. 45 + 99 = _____

18. 50 + 99 = _____

19. 75 + 99 = _____

20. 80 + 99 = _____

21. What is the result when 99 is added to a number?

_____

Name _____

Problem Solving
Too Much or Too Little Information

Write **a** or **b** to tell whether the problem has
a. too much information.   **b.** too little information.
Then solve if possible.

1. José ate 35 peanuts during the first show. How many peanuts did he eat during both shows?

_____

2. The lions' home is a 54-acre grassland. The tigers' area is 48 acres. There are 325 acres in the zoo. How many acres do the lions and tigers have in all?

_____

3. A zookeeper's manual has 210 pages. There are 37 pages on feeding, 49 pages on care, and 83 pages on rules. How many pages are there on feeding and care combined?

_____

4. One bus bringing zoo visitors has 55 students. Another bus contains more students. How many students are there altogether?

_____

Mixed Applications ▷ **STRATEGIES**   • Act It Out • Guess and Check
• Write a Number Sentence • Use a Table

Choose a strategy and solve.

5. Jo Ito fed 10 fish to the seals. He threw 4 fish right into a seal's mouth. How many times did he miss a seal's mouth?

_____

6. Leo the lion is 7 years older than Lori the lion, who is 9 years old. How old is Leo?

_____

WRITER'S CORNER

7. Describe how you solved Exercise 5 or Exercise 6.

_____

_____

Name _____

Subtracting One- and Two-Digit Numbers

Estimate the difference by rounding. Show your work.

1. 98 _____
    − 29 − _____
    _____

2. 51 _____
    − 18 − _____
    _____

3. 82 _____
    − 41 − _____
    _____

4. 72 _____
    − 8 − _____
    _____

Find the difference.

5. 83
    − 67

6. 75
    − 54

7. 37
    − 19

8. 93
    − 56

9. 87
    − 27

10. 48
    − 39

11. 92
    − 48

12. 71
    − 48

13. 70
    − 18

14. 88
    − 78

15. 68
    − 40

16. 34
    − 29

Mixed Applications

17. Tickets to the circus cost $15 for adults and $8 for children. How much will it cost for a family of two adults and one child to go to the circus?

    _____

18. Bill can buy popcorn for 39¢ or peanuts for 75¢. How much more do peanuts cost than popcorn?

    _____

EVERYDAY MATH CONNECTION

peanuts 39¢   popcorn 25¢   drink 15¢   hot dog 50¢

19. Choose two different snacks to buy. Ring them.

    What is the total cost? _____

    How much change would you get from 95¢? _____

HBJ material copyrighted under notice appearing earlier in this work.

Name _____

Subtracting with Zeros

■■■■■■■■ 3.7
■ USE WHAT YOU
■ KNOW
■■■■■■■■■■

Estimate the difference.

1. 60 −29	2. 50 − 11	3. 40 − 32	4. 90 − 58	5. 80 − 79	6. 70 − 41

Find the difference. Check by adding.

7. 90 ____ − 23 + ____ ____	8. 50 ____ − 18 + ____ ____	9. 80 ____ − 46 + ____ ____	10. 70 ____ − 63 + ____ ____
11. 40 ____ − 17 + ____ ____	12. 60 ____ − 27 + ____ ____	13. 30 ____ − 19 + ____ ____	14. 90 ____ − 45 + ____ ____

Mixed Applications

15. The parrot house contains 56 parrots and 37 other colorful birds. How many birds are in the parrot house?

_____

16. In the flamingo garden, 17 of the 40 pink birds are wading in the shallow pond. How many flamingos are not wading?

_____

SCIENCE CONNECTION

17. Flamingos usually lay a single egg in a shallow hole at the top of a mound of mud. The parents take turns sitting on the egg to keep it warm. Last year at the wildlife park, one flamingo egg took 27 days to hatch and another egg took 32 days. What is the difference between the hatching times of the two eggs?

_____

Use with text pages 84–85.

P 31

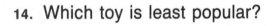 Name _____

Addition and Subtraction Practice

Find the sum or difference.

1. 23 +48	2. 57 +65	3. 98 −49	4. 86 −21	5. 91 +18	6. 37 − 9

7. 43 +59	8. 29 −12	9. 81 −56	10. 76 +76	11. 83 −47	12. 21 +99

Mixed Applications

Use the table to solve.

Toy	Number Sold
balloon	2,508
stuffed lion	1,897
banner	980
circus visor	2,256

13. Which circus toy is the best seller?

_____

14. Which toy is least popular?

_____

15. Which toys have sales of about 2,000?

_____

_____

16. Put the sales of stuffed lions, banners, and circus visors in order from highest to lowest.

_____

_____

WRITER'S CORNER

17. Make up your own question about the data in the table. Have a partner find the answer.

_____

_____

Use with text pages 86–87.

Problem Solving
Organize Data

Maria made a table to show the number of photographs she took of different animals at the zoo.

Animal	Photographs	Number
reptiles	II	
monkeys	卌 II	
giraffes	II	
tigers	IIII	
pandas	卌 IIII	

1. Record the number of tally marks for each kind of animal.

2. Which kind of animal did Maria photograph the most?

_____

3. Which two kinds did Maria photograph the same number of times?

_____ and _____

4. How many fewer times did Maria photograph tigers than pandas?

_____

┌─────────────────────┐
│ **Mixed Applications** ▷ **STRATEGIES**   • Act It Out • Guess and Check
                                            •Write a Number Sentence • Use a Table

Choose a strategy and solve.

5. Out of a roll of 36 photographs, 27 are of animals. How many photographs are not of animals?

_____

6. Maria spent $0.85 for the bus, $4.15 for film, and $2.37 for lunch. Put her expenses in order from least to greatest.

_____

┌─────────────────┐
│ **MIXED REVIEW** │
└─────────────────┘

Write *even* or *odd*.

1. 45 _____   2. 21 _____   3. 421 _____   4. 978 _____

Write the next two numbers.

5. 43, 45, 47, 49, _____, _____   6. 75, 70, 65, 60, _____, _____

Estimating Sums

Estimate the sum by rounding.

1.	388 +412	2.	479 +596	3.	218 +195

4. 165
 +815

5. 321
 +780

6. 275
 +443

7. 867
 +759

8. 963
 +529

9. 648
 +265

10. 479
 +762

Estimate the sum by using the front digits.

11. 219
 +425

12. 617
 +189

13. 476
 +207

14. 246
 +713

15. 369
 +369

Mixed Applications

16. The subway trains carry 278 people to school each day. Another 113 people ride buses. To the nearest hundred, how many people ride buses and subways to school?

_____

17. The eastbound subway carries 489 passengers. The westbound train carries only 215 people. To the nearest hundred, how many people ride both trains?

_____

MIXED REVIEW

Solve.

1. 46
 +19

2. 31
 +15

3. 82
 −40

4. 58
 −29

5. 90
 +15

6. 67
 −17

7. Write in order from least to greatest.
 649; 4,122; 194

_____

8. Write in order from greatest to least.
 540, 450, 405

_____

9. Ring the odd numbers.

 693, 467, 392, 908

Name _____

Exploring Three-Digit Addition

Find the sum.

1. 268 + 409	2. 435 + 943	3. 119 + 605	4. 34 + 128	5. 263 + 144
6. 328 + 851	7. 768 + 126	8. 418 + 475	9. 689 + 410	10. 254 + 314
11. 209 + 68	12. 323 + 524	13. 353 + 139	14. 220 + 719	15. 293 + 546

16. In which exercises were the ones regrouped?

_____

17. In which exercises were the tens regrouped?

_____

18. In which exercises were the hundreds regrouped?

_____

19. In which exercises were none of the places regrouped?

_____

VISUAL THINKING

Find the sum. You may use place-value models to help you.

20.

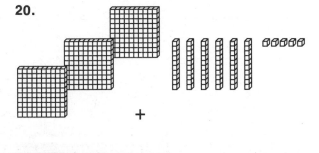

= _____

21.

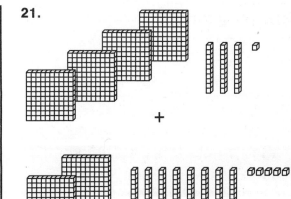

= _____

More Addition
Three-Digit Numbers

Find the sum.

1. 497 + 528	2. 883 + 684	3. 741 + 759	4. 942 + 489	5. 987 + 702

6. 468 123 + 372	7. 203 75 + 849	8. 452 268 + 173	9. 511 89 + 265	10. 496 145 + 306

11. 321 150 + 147	12. 53 675 + 219	13. 679 102 + 328	14. 825 319 + 89	15. 209 425 + 85

Mixed Applications

16. Train Treats sells 547 rolls and 665 bagels each morning to people riding the train to work. How many rolls and bagels do they sell?

_____

17. Train Treats orders 284 boxes of herbal tea. A supply of 549 boxes is already on hand. How many boxes will there be when the order comes in?

_____

HEALTH CONNECTION

18. Ming wants to do 100 push-ups each week. She had done 85 push-ups after 6 days, and just did 20 more on the seventh day. Did Ming reach her goal?

_____

19. Ron runs around the 440-yard track with his dad twice in one day. He runs it one time the next day. How many yards does Ron run in both days?

_____

Adding Money Amounts

Find the sum.

1. $3.14 + 3.75	2. $5.98 + 2.15	3. $4.15 + 6.89	4. $9.08 + .79	5. $6.18 + 4.25

6. $5.72 + 7.48	7. $3.61 + 8.68	8. $7.59 + 8.69	9. $8.93 + 8.87	10. $7.47 + 6.25

11. $5.63 + $8.96 = _____   12. $9.90 + $2.47 = _____

13. $4.82 + $2.99 = _____   14. $5.83 + $3.85 = _____

Mixed Applications

15. Rita rides the bus to and from work each day. The fare each way is $2.20. How much does Rita spend on bus fare each day?

_____

16. Roberto spends $1.75 on the eastbound bus. Then he transfers to the southbound bus and pays $2.90. Is his total fare more than or less than $5.00?

_____

| LOGICAL REASONING |
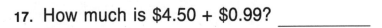

Solve using mental math.
Use the fact **$4.50 + $1.00 = $5.50** to help you.

17. How much is $4.50 + $0.99? _____

18. How much is $4.50 + $1.05? _____

19. How much is $4.50 + $2.00? _____

20. How much is $4.50 + $0.95? _____

Estimating Differences

Estimate the difference by rounding.

1. 588 −412	2. 979 −596	3. 818 −295	4. 885 −215	5. 621 −409
6. 589 −243	7. 897 − 95	8. 963 −269	9. 895 −285	10. 679 −398

Estimate the difference by using the front digits.

11. 819 −425	12. 617 −119	13. 476 −207	14. 608 −348	15. 969 −416

Mixed Applications

16. The Smiths are driving to the beach. They have traveled 284 miles out of a 615-mile trip. To the nearest hundred, how many more miles must they travel?

_____

17. The Smiths stop after every 225 miles so the family can stretch. Their last stop was 487 miles into the trip. About how many miles into their trip will they stop next?

_____

WRITER'S CORNER

18. Use the facts to write an estimation problem.

Dallas ↔ St. Louis: 630 miles
Dallas ↔ Tulsa: 257 miles
St. Louis ↔ Denver: 857 miles

_____

_____

_____

Subtracting Three-Digit Numbers

Find the difference. Check by adding. Show your work.

1. 861 _____   2. 853 _____   3. 590 _____   4. 748 _____
    − 644 + _____   − 427 + _____   − 46 + _____   − 145 + _____

    _____   _____   _____   _____

Find the difference.

5. 870   6. 965   7. 785   8. 973   9. 697
    − 543   − 247   − 183   − 48   − 160

10. 375   11. 892   12. 660   13. 897   14. 768
    − 125   − 537   − 435   − 369   − 265

Mixed Applications

15. A taxi driver travels 480 miles in Week 1 and 612 miles in Week 2. How many more miles does he drive in Week 2?

    _____

16. An airport van service took 367 people to Kennedy Airport and 595 people to LaGuardia Airport. How many people did the van service take to the two airports?

    _____

LOGICAL REASONING

Ring exercises that have estimated sums or differences greater than 500. Check your estimates with a calculator.

17. 398   18. 879   19. 312   20. 723   21. 442
    + 157   − 389   + 149   − 119   + 89

Problem Solving
Choose the Operation

Tell whether you need to add or subtract. Then solve.

1. A travel book contains 187 pages of maps. The rest of the 490-page book contains data about each U.S. city. How many pages are not maps?

   _____

2. The travel book describes 597 inns and 259 motels in a large city. How many inns and motels are described for the city?

   _____

Mixed Applications ⟩ **STRATEGIES**

• Act It Out • Guess and Check
• Use a Table

Choose a strategy and solve.

3. Yoko pays $2.49 for cereal and juice in a hotel coffee shop. A local diner charges $1.75 for cereal and juice. How much less expensive is the meal at the diner?

   _____

4. Molly is 7 years older than Ted. Ted is 5 years older than Brenda. Ted is 7 years old. How old are Molly and Brenda?

   _____

   _____

5. Mr. Carr is 6 years older than Mrs. Carr. The sum of their ages is 78. How old are each of them?

   _____

6. Dan did his math homework before his spelling. He did his reading homework after his spelling. He did his science homework before his math. What did he do last?

   _____

   _____

LOGICAL REASONING

7. Write three subtraction examples that each have a difference of 111. Describe the pattern you see.

   ____   ____   ____
   −____   −____   −____
   111   111   111

Subtracting
Regroup Tens and Hundreds

Find the difference.

1. 546 − 459	**2.** 949 − 368	**3.** 815 − 438	**4.** 746 − 209	**5.** 912 − 798
6. 869 − 679	**7.** 452 − 317	**8.** 546 − 281	**9.** 515 − 495	**10.** 728 − 384

11. 219 − 68 = _____   **12.** 489 − 392 = _____

Mixed Applications

13. In June, Hank jogged 181 miles and Marcie jogged 214 miles. How many more miles did Marcie jog than Hank?

_____

14. Marcie jogged 214 miles in June, 197 miles in July, and 84 miles in August. How many miles did she jog in the 3-month period?

_____

NUMBER SENSE

15. Complete the numbers to form two 3-digit odd numbers and two 3-digit even numbers.

7 _ _   2 _ _   3 _ _   6 _ _
odd   odd   even   even

Use the numbers you wrote to solve. Write *odd* or *even* beside the difference.

even 6 _ _	even 6 _ _	odd 7 _ _	odd 7 _ _
− even − 3 _ _	− odd − 2 _ _	− odd − 2 _ _	− even − _____
_____	_____	_____	_____

Exploring Subtraction with Zeros

Use place-value models. Regroup to solve each problem. Choose **a, b,** or **c** to show how you regrouped.

1. 503
  − 258

a.
H	T	O
4	10	13

b.
H	T	O
4	9	13

c.
H	T	O
3	9	10

2. 800
  − 349

a.
H	T	O
7	10	10

b.
H	T	O
7	9	10

c.
H	T	O
8	9	10

3. 602
  − 498

a.
H	T	O
5	10	12

b.
H	T	O
6	9	12

c.
H	T	O
5	9	12

4. 960
  − 386

a.
H	T	O
8	15	10

b.
H	T	O
8	15	0

c.
H	T	O
8	16	10

5. 610
  − 492

a.
H	T	O
6	9	10

b.
H	T	O
5	9	10

c.
H	T	O
5	10	10

MIXED REVIEW

Tell the value of the digit **7** in each number.

1. 47,819 _____

2. 703,124 _____

3. 1,798 _____

4. 670,253 _____

Subtracting Across Zeros

Find the difference.

1. 508	2. 900	3. 807	4. 800	5. 609
− 412	− 376	− 295	− 478	− 597

6. 501	7. 203	8. 904	9. 703	10. 600
− 347	− 95	− 369	− 285	− 401

Use mental math to solve each problem.

11. $800 - 300 =$ _____

12. $700 -$ _____ $= 300$

13. $900 -$ _____ $= 700$

14. $600 - 400 =$ _____

Mixed Applications

15. A sports car can go 192 kilometers per hour, but the top speed allowed on most U.S. highways is 88 kilometers per hour. How many more kilometers per hour can the car travel than it is allowed to?

_____

16. The total distance of a car race is 800 kilometers. If a car racer has traveled 489 kilometers, how many more kilometers must he drive to complete the race?

_____

VISUAL THINKING

17. Draw a picture to show how you would use place-value models to solve the problem 703 − 289. Then solve.

703
− 289

Addition and Subtraction

Calculator

Use a calculator or paper and pencil to find the sum
or difference.

1. 781
  + 397

2. 1,075
  − 379

3. 4,904
  + 2,097

4. 803
  − 157

5.   798
  + 4,806

. 3,097 + 5,219 = _____

7. 6,004 − 1,997 = _____

Mixed Applications

newspaper magazine book puzzlers comic books
$0.50 $2.95 $5.95 $3.75 $1.59

8. How much change do you get
   from $5.00 if you buy a
   magazine?

   _____

9. How much change do you get
   from $9.00 if you buy a book
   and a magazine?

   _____

10. How much do puzzlers, a
    newspaper, and a book cost?

    _____

11. How much more is a book of
    puzzlers than a magazine?

    _____

CONSUMER CONNECTION

12. Choose two items from the newsstand to buy.
    Find the total cost and the change you would get
    from $10.00. You may use a calculator.

Item	Cost	Change from $10

Problem-Solving Strategy
Write a Number Sentence

Write a number sentence. Solve.

1. Scott rides his bike 4 miles on Friday, 8 miles on Saturday, and 7 miles on Sunday. How many miles does Scott ride in the three days?

_____

2. Shea rides along a 16-mile bike path. She has ridden 9 miles so far. How many more miles will Shea ride until she reaches the end of the path?

_____

Mixed Applications ⟩ **STRATEGIES**

• Act It Out • Guess and Check
•Use a Table
• Write a Number Sentence

Choose a strategy and solve.

3. Caroline rides her bike 3 miles farther than Jo. Together, they ride 25 miles. How many miles does each girl ride?

_____

4. In a bike race, Arthur is behind Violet. Mel is ahead of Chip. Mel is between Arthur and Chip. What is the order of the children in the race?

_____

5. Carlos bought a bike horn for $5.97 and a bike tail light for $3.79. Did Carlos spend more or less than $10.00? How much more or less?

_____

6. Miguel bought a pair of handlebar ribbons for his bike. He received $1.82 change from $5.00. How much did the ribbons cost?

_____

VISUAL THINKING

7. A bike path is shaped like a triangle. Two long sides are 5 miles each, and the length of the short side is 3 miles. What is the total distance around the path? Write a number sentence. Solve.

_____

Name _____

Using a Calendar

Use the calendar for Exercises 1–9.
Write the day of the week.

1. April 5   **2.** April 15

_____   _____

Write the date one week before.

3. April 27   **4.** April 12

_____   _____

APRIL						
S	M	T	W	T	F	S
				1	2	3
4	5	6	7	8	9	10
11	12	13	14	15	16	17
18	19	20	21	22	23	24
25	26	27	28	29	30	

5. How many days are in April?

_____

6. What is the date of the second Wednesday?

_____

7. If April ends on a Friday, on what day does May begin?

_____

Mixed Applications

8. Jessica's tap recital is on April 12. Today is April 3. How many days are there until the recital?

_____

9. Tap class takes a two-week break beginning April 14. On what day do classes begin again?

_____

VISUAL THINKING

10. February 12th and March 12th fall on the same day of the week. In fact, all of the dates in each month fall on the same day. How can you explain that?

_____

_____

FEBRUARY						
S	M	T	W	T	F	S
	1	2	3	4	5	6
7	8	9	10	11	12	13
14	15	16	17	18	19	20
21	22	23	24	25	26	27
28						

MARCH						
S	M	T	W	T	F	S
	1	2	3	4	5	6
7	8	9	10	11	12	13
14	15	16	17	18	19	20
21	22	23	24	25	26	27
28	29	30	31			

Use with text pages 132–133.

Understanding Minutes and Hours

Ring the activity that will take longer.

1. to eat breakfast   or   to watch a movie

2. to read a book   or   to brush your teeth

3. to make your bed   or   to sneeze

Ring the better estimate.

4. to attend your classes   6 minutes   or   6 hours

5. to wash a load of laundry   4 minutes   or   40 minutes

Decide whether the estimated time in each sentence is reasonable. Write *yes* or *no.*

6. It takes about 1 minute to sharpen a pencil. _____

7. Eating a sandwich takes about 3 hours. _____

Mixed Applications

8. Deena swam across the pool. Did it take about *2 minutes* or about *2 hours?*

   _____

9. Mrs. Rios knitted a red, white, and blue scarf. Did it take about *15 minutes* or about *15 hours?*

   _____

| WRITER'S CORNER |
---

10. How can you explain the saying "Time flies when you're having fun"?

_____

_____

_____

Name _____

Exploring Using a Clock

Write the time for each clockface.

1.

_____

2.

_____

3.

_____

Begin at the 12. Write how many minutes the minute hand has moved. Count by fives. Use your clockface.

4.

_____

5.

_____

6.

_____

Mixed Applications

7. When Fay's mother asked what time it was, Fay told her that the minute hand was on the 12 and the hour hand was on the 3. What time was it?

_____

8. The minute hand on Fay's clock was on the 8. Fay's mother said they would leave for the park in 5 minutes. Where will the minute hand be then?

_____

MIXED REVIEW

Find the sum or difference.

1. 590
   + 42

2. 801
   − 275

3. 4,980
   + 2,378

4. 3,140
   − 2,001

5. 4,897
   + 4,987

Time After the Hour

Use your clockface.

A.

B.

C.

Clock A   Clock B   Clock C

1. Write the time shown on each clock.

2. Write the time 1 hour later than shown.

3. Write the time 30 minutes later than shown.

4. Write the time 15 minutes later than shown.

Mixed Applications

Use your clockface. Solve.

5. Nathan's party began at 2:30. It lasted for 1 hour. At what time was the party over?

6. The children started playing games at 2:45. They played for 30 minutes. At what time did they stop playing?

___

EVERYDAY MATH CONNECTION

Write the time as you would see it on a digital clock.
Then write the words that tell the time.

7.

⎡ : ⎤

8.

⎡ : ⎤

9.

⎡ : ⎤

Exploring Time to the Minute

Count by fives to show the minutes that have passed from the first clock to the second clock.

1.

5, ____ , ____ , ____

2.

5, ____ , ____ , ____

3.

5, ____ , ____ , ____ , ____ , ____

4.

5, ____ , ____ , ____

Write the time 9 minutes later.

5.

_____

6.

_____

7.

_____

VISUAL THINKING

Draw the hands on each analog clock to match the time shown on the digital clock.

8.

9.

10.

```
4:25
```

```
1:55
```

```
9:11
```

Use with text pages 140–141.

Using a Schedule

Use the gymnasium
schedule for Exercises 1–6.

Gymnasium Schedule	
Time	Activity
3:30–4:15	Jr. Girls' Basketball
4:30–5:15	Jr. Boys' Basketball
5:30–6:30	Aerobics
6:45–7:30	Men's Basketball

1. Sean is a 9-year-old boy. At
   what time does his basketball
   practice begin?

   _____

2. Tom is a 35-year-old man. At
   what time does his basketball
   practice begin?

   _____

3. Which activity is taking place at
   7:00?

   _____

4. At what time is Luisa's aerobics
   class over?

   _____

5. How long is the aerobics class?

   _____

6. How long is each of the
   basketball classes?

   _____

Mixed Applications

7. Thad was 15 minutes late to
   basketball practice. If it began
   at 6:35, at what time did Thad
   arrive?

   _____

8. There are 129 boys and 216
   girls watching the basketball
   game. How many boys and
   girls are watching?

   _____

EVERYDAY MATH CONNECTION

9. Write your school schedule for
   today. Tell the time you will
   have reading and math. Tell
   the time you will have lunch
   and recess.

Time	Activity
_____	_____
_____	_____
_____	_____
_____	_____
_____	_____

Problem-Solving Strategy
Work Backward

Solve. Use your clockface.

1. Pablo got to the camp-out 1 hour late. The time was 10:15. When did the camp-out begin?

   _____

2. Martin spent 2 hours and 15 minutes in the library. He left the library at 4:30. At what time did he arrive?

   _____

3. Jeff returned from his errands at 2:00. He had been gone for 2 hours and 30 minutes. At what time did he leave?

   _____

4. Rosa thought of a number and added 5. She subtracted 3 and doubled her answer. What number did she begin with if her answer was 10?

   _____

Mixed Applications > **STRATEGIES**   • Act It Out • Work Backward
• Guess and Check • Draw a Picture

Choose a strategy and solve.

5. Sue must be home by 3:30. It takes 45 minutes to get home from the mall. At what time must Sue leave the mall?

   _____

6. The Kopps pose for a family picture. Debra is beside Matt. Len is between Debra and Andy. Andy is on the left end. How are they arranged?

   _____

EVERYDAY MATH CONNECTION

Write *hours* or *minutes* to complete each sentence.

7. Lauren does homework for 30 _____ each night.

8. Mike is at school for 6 _____ each weekday.

9. Carlota has art class for 45 _____ each week.

10. Yoshi runs 1 mile in 10 _____ .

Name _____

Counting Coins

Write the amount.

1. 1 quarter
   2 dimes
   3 pennies
   _____

2. 2 quarters
   1 dime
   4 nickels
   _____

3. 1 quarter
   3 nickels
   8 pennies
   _____

4. 3 quarters
   1 nickel
   6 pennies
   _____

Use play money to show one way to make each
amount. List the coins you use.

5. 83¢ _____

6. 47¢ _____

7. 65¢ _____

Mixed Applications

8. Kung has 3 quarters, 1 dime,
   and 4 pennies. How much
   money does he have?

   _____

9. Yana has 4 coins in her purse.
   They total 52¢. She has no
   dimes or nickels. What coins
   are in Yana's purse?

   _____

VISUAL THINKING

10.

Arch has these coins in his pocket. Write *yes* or
no to tell what he can buy.

_____   _____   _____   _____

Name _____

Counting Bills and Coins

Count the money and write the amount.

1.

_____

2.

_____

3.

_____

4.

_____

5.

_____

6.

_____

Mixed Applications

Use the picture for Exercises 7–9.

7. Delinda has three $1 bills, 3 quarters, and 2 pennies. Does she have enough money to buy the crayons?

_____

8. Carmen has four $1 bills, 2 quarters, 1 nickel, and 2 pennies. She buys the markers and the pencils. What coins does she have left?

_____

NUMBER SENSE

9. Ben buys the crayons and the pencils. He pays for his purchase with 5 bills and 5 coins. What bills and coins are they?

_____

Use with text pages 150–151.

Comparing Amounts of Money

Ring the letter of the matching amount.

1.    a.    b.    c.

2.    a.    b.    c.

Mixed Applications

3. A chess set costs $6.49. Gilda has one $5 bill, one $1 bill, and 4 nickels. How much more money does she need?

_____

4. Hans earns $5.00 baby-sitting. He wants to buy a board game for $3.95 and a comic book for $0.75. Does he have enough money?

_____

5. Lani has one $5 bill, two $1 bills, 3 quarters, 3 dimes, and 4 pennies. Can she buy a book for $6.95?

_____

6. Wes wants to buy a kite for $5.49, string for $2.25, and ribbon for $1.79. How much do the three items costs?

_____

MIXED REVIEW

Find the sum or difference.

1. $5.95	2. $2.97	3. $8.00	4. $9.70	5. $6.59
+ 1.79	+ 8.25	− 2.49	+ 2.43	− 4.95

Name _____

Exploring Counting Change

5.11

USE WHAT YOU KNOW

Use your play money. List the coins and bills you would receive in change.

	Paid	Cost of Item	Change
1.		$0.42	_____
2.		$0.78	_____
3.		 $2.47	_____

Use your play money. List the least number and type of coins you would receive in change from a $1 bill.

4.		5.	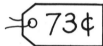	6.	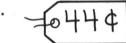

4. _____
_____

5. _____
_____

6. _____
_____

7. Bart bought a gift for $7.79. He gave the clerk a $10 bill. How much change should he receive?

_____

8. Maggie is saving $0.25 each week to buy a poster for $4.00. She has 15 quarters now. When will she have enough to buy the poster?

_____

LOGICAL REASONING

_____

List 4 coins that will give each value exactly.

9. 31¢ _____
_____

10. 40¢ _____
_____

11. 41¢ _____
_____

12. $1.00 _____
_____

Use with text pages 154–155.

Problem-Solving Strategy
Act It Out

Use play money to solve.

1. Ima bought a pen for $1.29.
   She paid for it with 9 coins.
   What coins did she use?

   _____

   _____

2. Lucia bought a cassette tape
   for $5.95. List two combinations
   of bills and coins she could use
   to pay for the cassette tape.

   _____

   _____

   _____

   _____

Mixed Applications > | STRATEGIES | • Guess and Check • Work Backward
• Act It Out • Draw a Picture
• Write a Number Sentence |

Choose a strategy and solve.

3. Mel had $9.42 in the bank. He
   added the $4.50 that he earned
   mowing the lawn. How much
   does Mel have in the bank now?

   _____

4. Dom paid for a magazine with
   a $10 bill. His change was
   $6.84. How much did the
   magazine cost?

   _____

5. Lani collects dimes. On Monday
   she added 7 dimes to her bank.
   Then she spent 5 dimes. Lani has
   12 dimes now. How many did she
   have to begin with?

   _____

6. Carol bought a puzzle book for
   $1.80. She gave the clerk 9 coins.
   What coins did Carol use?

   _____

   _____

EVERYDAY MATH CONNECTION

7. Write the amounts that show how a clerk would
   count 5 coins as the change from $1.34 to $2.00.

   _____   _____   _____   _____   _____

Exploring Addition and Multiplication

Use counters to help you find the totals.

1. 3
    +3

2. 5
    5
    +5

3. 7
    +7

4. 2
    2
    +2

2 threes = ___   3 fives = ___   2 sevens = ___   3 twos = ___

Use counters. Solve.

5. José has 3 rows of 2 animal cards on the table. Add or multiply to find out how many cards José has.

    _____

6. Hannah arranges her stickers in 4 rows of 3. Add or multiply to find out how many stickers Hannah has.

    _____

Draw a picture for each number sentence. Solve.

7. 4
    4
    +4

8. 6
    6
    +6

9. 7
    7
    +7

3 fours = ___   3 sixes = ___   3 sevens = ___

VISUAL THINKING

10. Ring the addition sentence and the multiplication sentence that tell about the picture.

3 + 3 = 6   2 + 4 = 6   4 + 4 = 8   4 + 2 = 6

2 threes = 6   2 fours = 8   4 twos = 8   1 eight = 8

Name _____

Connecting Addition and Multiplication

Write the addition sentence and the multiplication sentence for each picture.

1. ☆☆☆☆   ☆☆☆☆
   ☆☆☆☆   ☆☆☆☆

_____

2. △△△ △△△ △△△
   △△△ △△△ △△△

_____

Draw a picture for each multiplication sentence.

3. $4 \times 4 = 16$

4. $3 \times 3 = 9$

5. $5 \times 5 = 25$

Mixed Applications

Use counters. Solve.

6. Pete lines up his model airplanes in 5 rows. Each row has 3 airplanes. How many airplanes does Pete have?

_____

7. Each of 4 boys bought a 4-pack of mini-cars. Write an addition sentence and a multiplication sentence to show how many mini-cars they bought.

_____

_____

EVERYDAY MATH CONNECTION

_____

A nickel is worth 5¢. The value of a group of nickels can be found by adding or multiplying. Write an addition sentence and a multiplication sentence to tell the value of each group of nickels.

8.

9.

_____

_____

Multiplication Sentences

Use the number line. Write the addition number
sentence. Write the multiplication number sentence.

1.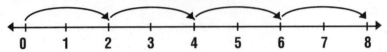

_____ _____

2.

_____ _____

3.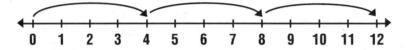

_____ _____

Mixed Applications

Show each problem on the number line. Solve.

4. Cass has 6 dolls from each
country her uncle has visited. He
has been to 3 countries. How
many dolls does Cass have?

_____

5. Four students each have 5 rare
pennies in their coin collections.
How many rare pennies do they
have?

_____

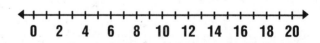

ART CONNECTION _____

6. Fold a piece of plain paper in half.
Fold it in half again, and in half one
more time. Unfold the paper. Draw
2 dots in each section. Write a
multiplication sentence to tell about
the dots. Show it on the number line.

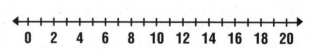

_____

Name _____

Multiply Using 2 as a Factor

Complete the multiplication sentence for each picture.

1.
   5 × 2 = _____

2. 6 × 2 = _____

3. 2 × 8 = _____

Write the multiplication sentence for each picture.

4.

5.

6.

_____

_____

_____

Find the product. You may draw a picture or use a number line.

7. 2
   ×5
   ———

8. 9
   ×2
   ———

9. 4
   ×2
   ———

10. 7
   ×2
   ———

11. 2
   ×8
   ———

12. 2
   ×6
   ———

Mixed Applications

Write a number sentence. Solve.

13. Sal has 6 rosebushes. He picks 2 roses from each bush. How many roses does he pick?

_____

14. Sal buys 24 pansies, 36 begonias, and 48 violas. How many flowers does Sal buy?

_____

| **LOGICAL REASONING** |

15. Luci, Juana, and Marco collect postcards when they go on trips. Luci has 3 fewer postcards than Juana. Marco has collected 5 postcards on each of 2 different trips. Juana has 2 times as many postcards as Marco. How many postcards does each person have?

_____

Use with text pages 172–173.

Problem-Solving Strategy
Find a Pattern

1. Find the next three numbers in the pattern: 23, 28, 33, 38, 43, 48, 53, ___, ___, ___ .

   _____

2. Rita places her dolls in a pattern of baby, baby, mama, baby, baby, mama, baby, baby, mama. What kinds of dolls are the next three in line?

   _____

Mixed Applications ⟩ **STRATEGIES** • Act It Out • Guess and Check • Find a Pattern • Write a Number Sentence

Choose a strategy and solve.

3. Barbra has 3 dolls. Each doll has 5 outfits. How many outfits does Barbra have for her dolls?

   _____

4. Draw the next five shapes in the pattern.
   □□□○○□□□○○

   _____

5. The days on a calendar make a pattern. If May 4 is a Wednesday, what day of the week is May 11?

   _____

6. Chico has one $1 bill and one quarter. How much money does Chico have? Can he buy a lunch that costs $1.20?

   _____

MIXED REVIEW

Round each number to the nearest hundred and estimate the sum or difference.

1. 397 +215	2. 413 −295	3. 683 +106	4. 209 − 84	5. 828 +861

Write the time.

6. _____

7.  _____

Use with text pages 174–175.

Name _____

Multiply Using 3 as a Factor

Use the number line to find the product.

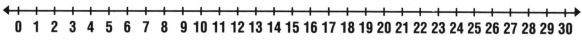

0 1 2 3 4 5 6 7 8 9 10 11 12 13 14 15 16 17 18 19 20 21 22 23 24 25 26 27 28 29 30

1. $3 \times 8 =$ ___   **2.** $4 \times 3 =$ ___   **3.** $3 \times 6 =$ ___

Write the multiplication sentence for each picture.

4.

5.

6.

_____   _____   _____

Find the product.

7. 2
$\times 3$

8. 9
$\times 3$

9. 3
$\times 8$

10. 7
$\times 3$

11. 3
$\times 5$

12. 3
$\times 6$

Mixed Applications

13. There are 5 shelves of footballs in a closet. Each shelf has 3 footballs. How many footballs are there?

_____

14. Kiri hunts lost golf balls. She finds 16 balls near the clubhouse. She finds 6 in one sandtrap, 9 in another trap, and 10 in the bushes. How many golf balls did she find?

_____

| VISUAL THINKING |

Draw number lines to help you solve.

15. José and Edward each filled a photo album. Edward said he had more photos than José because his album had 4 pages more than José's. José said he had more photos because he put 6 photos on each of the 5 pages in his album and Edward put 4 on each page. Which boy was right? How many photos did each boy have?

_____

Multiply Using 4 as a Factor

Draw a picture for each multiplication sentence.
Solve.

1. $8 \times 4 =$ ___

2. $2 \times 4 =$ ___

3. $7 \times 4 =$ ___

Find the product.

4. $\begin{array}{r} 8 \\ \times 3 \\ \hline \end{array}$

5. $\begin{array}{r} 3 \\ \times 9 \\ \hline \end{array}$

6. $\begin{array}{r} 2 \\ \times 4 \\ \hline \end{array}$

7. $\begin{array}{r} 7 \\ \times 4 \\ \hline \end{array}$

8. $\begin{array}{r} 4 \\ \times 9 \\ \hline \end{array}$

9. $\begin{array}{r} 3 \\ \times 7 \\ \hline \end{array}$

10. $3 \times 3 =$ ___

11. $4 \times 6 =$ ___

12. $4 \times 4 =$ ___

13. $4 \times 5 =$ ___

Mixed Applications

14. Mabel buys 6 cards with animal buttons on them. Each card has 4 buttons. How many animal buttons does Mabel buy?

_____

15. Jen sews animal buttons on her clothes. She puts 4 tigers on her shirt, 3 giraffes on her hat, 16 seals on her skirt, and 1 lion on each glove. How many animal buttons does she sew?

_____

EVERYDAY MATH CONNECTION

In our money system, four quarters equal one dollar. Tell how many quarters equal each group of dollars.

16. $2 = ___ quarters

17. $3 = ___ quarters

18. $4 = ___ quarters

Use with text pages 180–181.

Multiply Using 5 as a Factor

Draw a picture for each multiplication sentence.
Solve.

1. $4 \times 5 =$ ___

2. $3 \times 5 =$ ___

3. $6 \times 5 =$ ___

Find the product.

4. $8 \times 5 =$ ___

5. $2 \times 5 =$ ___

6. $7 \times 5 =$ ___

7. $5 \times 5 =$ ___

8. $\begin{array}{r} 5 \\ \times 9 \\ \hline \end{array}$

9. $\begin{array}{r} 7 \\ \times 4 \\ \hline \end{array}$

10. $\begin{array}{r} 5 \\ \times 1 \\ \hline \end{array}$

11. $\begin{array}{r} 8 \\ \times 3 \\ \hline \end{array}$

12. $\begin{array}{r} 9 \\ \times 4 \\ \hline \end{array}$

13. $\begin{array}{r} 4 \\ \times 5 \\ \hline \end{array}$

Write $+$, $-$, or $\times$ for each $\bigcirc$.

14. $5 \bigcirc 3 = 8$

15. $5 \bigcirc 3 = 15$

16. $5 \bigcirc 3 = 2$

Mixed Applications

17. Jiro needs 5 nickels to pay for a pack of baseball cards. Write a multiplication sentence to find the cost.

_____

18. Milo gave the clerk a $1 bill. The clerk gave Milo 4 dimes in change. How much change did Milo get? How much was his purchase?

_____

_____

NUMBER SENSE

Solve the number puzzles.

19. One of my factors is 5. My product is 30. What is my other number?

_____

20. My factors are both the same. My product is 25. What are my factors?

_____

Multiply Using 1 and 0 as Factors

Find the product.

1. $9 \times 0 =$ ___

2. $8 \times 1 =$ ___

3. $4 \times 0 =$ ___

4. $7 \times 1 =$ ___

5. $6 \times 0 =$ ___

6. $3 \times 1 =$ ___

7. $9 \times 1 =$ ___

8. $10 \times 0 =$ ___

9. $8 \times 0 =$ ___

10. $10 \times 1 =$ ___

11. $7 \times 0 =$ ___

12. $6 \times 1 =$ ___

13. $\begin{array}{r} 4 \\ \times 0 \\ \hline \end{array}$

14. $\begin{array}{r} 3 \\ \times 1 \\ \hline \end{array}$

15. $\begin{array}{r} 2 \\ \times 0 \\ \hline \end{array}$

16. $\begin{array}{r} 9 \\ \times 0 \\ \hline \end{array}$

17. $\begin{array}{r} 1 \\ \times 1 \\ \hline \end{array}$

18. $\begin{array}{r} 0 \\ \times 8 \\ \hline \end{array}$

19. $\begin{array}{r} 5 \\ \times 1 \\ \hline \end{array}$

20. $\begin{array}{r} 3 \\ \times 0 \\ \hline \end{array}$

21. $\begin{array}{r} 4 \\ \times 1 \\ \hline \end{array}$

22. $\begin{array}{r} 2 \\ \times 0 \\ \hline \end{array}$

23. $\begin{array}{r} 0 \\ \times 5 \\ \hline \end{array}$

24. $\begin{array}{r} 1 \\ \times 2 \\ \hline \end{array}$

Mixed Applications

25. Marie put 1 sticker on each page of her 8-page sticker album. How many stickers did Marie put in her album?

_____

26. Inez has 37 fuzzy stickers and 61 scented stickers. How many more scented stickers than fuzzy stickers does Inez have?

_____

MIXED REVIEW

Write each number in stan dard form.

1. four hundred twenty-three thousand, sixteen

_____

2. ninety-seven thousand, one hundred thirty

_____

3. $800,000 + 40,000 + 600 + 30 + 1$

_____

4. $200,000 + 2,000 + 20$

_____

Problem Solving
Choose a Strategy

Mixed Applications ⟩	STRATEGIES	• Act It Out • Make a Model • Work Backward • Write a Number Sentence

Choose a strategy and solve.

1. Hector covered a wall using 1-foot mirror squares. The wall is 3 feet wide and 7 feet long. How many 1-foot squares did Hector use?

   _____

2. Abby made a tapestry design out of 16 square fabric samples. The design is in the shape of a square. Make a model of the design. Draw your model in the space below.

   _____

3. A large window is made up of square panes. The window is 4 panes wide and 8 panes long. How many panes make up the large window?

   _____

4. Mae, Sue, Bob, and Pete each bought a 5-sticker sheet. How many stickers did they have among them?

   _____

5. Tani spent 45 minutes in the mall. He left the mall at 2:30. At what time did he arrive at the mall?

   _____

WRITER'S CORNER

6. Write a problem that can be solved using the *make a model* strategy. Exchange with a classmate and solve.

   _____

   _____

Name _____

Mental Math:
Reviewing Facts 0–5

Find the product.

1. 4 ×3	2. 3 ×7	3. 5 ×2	4. 7 ×2	5. 8 ×3	6. 2 ×9

7. 4 ×8	8. 5 ×5	9. 3 ×3	10. 6 ×2	11. 2 ×8	12. 6 ×3

13. $2 \times 6 =$ ___   14. $3 \times 9 =$ ___   15. $4 \times 5 =$ ___   16. $5 \times 3 =$ ___

17. $5 \times 6 =$ ___   18. $2 \times 5 =$ ___   19. $3 \times 4 =$ ___   20. $9 \times 5 =$ ___

Mixed Applications

21. Wes made 2 green rings. He made 3 times as many red rings. How many red rings did Wes make?

_____

22. The Craft Shop sells 5 times as many red mats as blue. The shop sold 4 blue mats today. How many red mats were sold?

_____

23. Yarn is on sale for 5¢ a skein. How much will 9 skeins cost?

_____

24. Moe buys 48 shells. Joy buys 15 shells more than Moe. How many shells does Joy buy?

_____

VISUAL THINKING

Write the multiplication fact for each picture.

25.

26.

_____   _____

Use with text pages 196–197.

Name _____

Exploring Arrays

Write the multiplication sentence for each array.

1. _____   2. _____   3. _____

4. _____   5. _____   6. _____

7. Look at your answers to Exercises 1–6. Write the
multiplication sentences with products that are
square numbers.

_____

Find the product. Write *yes* or *no* to tell which
products are square numbers.

8. 7	9. 3	10. 6	11. 6	12. 7	13. 8
×7	×8	×6	×5	×8	×8

___ ___ ___ ___ ___ ___

MIXED REVIEW

Find the sum or difference.

1. 396	2. 279	3. 1,230	4. 8,903	5. $5.90
+197	− 83	− 985	+2,468	− 1.79

Find the sum. Write the matching multiplication sentence.

6. $2 + 2 + 2 + 2 =$ _____   7. $5 + 5 + 5 + 5 + 5 =$ _____

_____   _____

Multiply
Using 6 as a Factor

Draw a number line to find the product.

1. $9 \times 6 =$ ___

2. $8 \times 6 =$ ___

3. $6 \times 5 =$ ___

4. $7 \times 6 =$ ___

Find the product.

5. $\begin{array}{r} 3 \\ \times 6 \\ \hline \end{array}$
6. $\begin{array}{r} 4 \\ \times 6 \\ \hline \end{array}$
7. $\begin{array}{r} 6 \\ \times 6 \\ \hline \end{array}$
8. $\begin{array}{r} 6 \\ \times 8 \\ \hline \end{array}$
9. $\begin{array}{r} 6 \\ \times 5 \\ \hline \end{array}$
10. $\begin{array}{r} 8 \\ \times 8 \\ \hline \end{array}$

11. $\begin{array}{r} 4 \\ \times 8 \\ \hline \end{array}$
12. $\begin{array}{r} 6 \\ \times 5 \\ \hline \end{array}$
13. $\begin{array}{r} 5 \\ \times 9 \\ \hline \end{array}$
14. $\begin{array}{r} 5 \\ \times 7 \\ \hline \end{array}$
15. $\begin{array}{r} 6 \\ \times 7 \\ \hline \end{array}$
16. $\begin{array}{r} 6 \\ \times 9 \\ \hline \end{array}$

Mixed Applications

Solve.

17. There are 8 cassette tapes on each of 6 shelves. How many tapes are on the shelves?

_____

18. Mary buys 6 tapes at $2.00 each and a case for $4.98. How much money does she spend?

_____

NUMBER SENSE

19. One factor is 5. The product is 35. What is the other factor?

_____

20. The product is 36. Both factors are the same. What are the factors?

_____

Use with text pages 200–201.

Multiply
Using 7 as a Factor

Use what you know about the Order Property to find the product.

1. $7 \times 9 =$ _____   2. $7 \times 3 =$ _____   3. $7 \times 2 =$ _____   4. $8 \times 7 =$ _____

5. $7 \times 6 =$ _____   6. $9 \times 7 =$ _____   7. $5 \times 7 =$ _____   8. $7 \times 4 =$ _____

Find the product.

9. $\begin{array}{r} 8 \\ \times 7 \\ \hline \end{array}$ 10. $\begin{array}{r} 7 \\ \times 3 \\ \hline \end{array}$ 11. $\begin{array}{r} 7 \\ \times 9 \\ \hline \end{array}$ 12. $\begin{array}{r} 9 \\ \times 3 \\ \hline \end{array}$ 13. $\begin{array}{r} 2 \\ \times 8 \\ \hline \end{array}$ 14. $\begin{array}{r} 4 \\ \times 6 \\ \hline \end{array}$

15. $\begin{array}{r} 4 \\ \times 9 \\ \hline \end{array}$ 16. $\begin{array}{r} 7 \\ \times 5 \\ \hline \end{array}$ 17. $\begin{array}{r} 6 \\ \times 3 \\ \hline \end{array}$ 18. $\begin{array}{r} 8 \\ \times 6 \\ \hline \end{array}$ 19. $\begin{array}{r} 7 \\ \times 7 \\ \hline \end{array}$ 20. $\begin{array}{r} 7 \\ \times 8 \\ \hline \end{array}$

Mixed Applications

Solve.

21. Risa buys a model for $6.75, paint for $1.98, and glue for $0.95. How much does Risa spend?

_____

22. Thuy puts 7 toy boats in each of 8 rows. How many boats does he have?

_____

EVERYDAY MATH CONNECTION

There are 7 days in 1 week.

23. A month is about 4 weeks long. About how many days is that?

_____

24. A year is about 52 weeks long. About how many days is that? Use your calculator to help you.

_____

1993						
S	M	T	W	T	F	S
January						
					1	2
3	4	5	6	7	8	9
10	11	12	13	14	15	16
17	18	19	20	21	22	23
24/31	25	26	27	28	29	30

Name _____

Multiply
Using 8 as a Factor

7.5

USE WHAT YOU KNOW

Complete the table. Find the product.

1.

×	0	1	2	3	4	5	6	7	8	9
8										

Find the product.

2. 8
   ×7

3. 4
   ×9

4. 8
   ×8

5. 5
   ×8

6. 9
   ×7

7. 8
   ×2

8. $8 \times 3 =$ _____

9. $9 \times 8 =$ _____

10. $4 \times 8 =$ _____

11. $6 \times 8 =$ _____

Mixed Applications

Solve.

12. Ellen buys toy rings at 8 for $1.00. She spends $3.00. How many toy rings does she buy?

_____

13. A plastic model costs $3.98. A metal model costs $6.75. How much more does a metal model cost than a plastic model?

_____

| **EVERYDAY MATH CONNECTION** |

The standard height of a 1-story room is 8 feet. A building that is 3 stories high may be about 24 feet tall, because $3 \times 8 = 24$.

Find about how tall each of these buildings is. Use your calculator when needed.

14. 5-story house = about _____ feet tall.

15. 8-story apartment house = about _____ feet tall.

16. 10-story hotel = about _____ feet tall.

17. 25-story skyscraper = about _____ feet tall.

72 ℗

Use with text pages 204–205.

HBJ material copyrighted under notice appearing earlier in this work.

Problem Solving
Too Much or Too Little Information

Write **a** if the problem has too much information. Then solve.
Write **b** if there is too little information to solve the problem.

1. Dean makes cookies to sell. He puts them in the oven at 2:30. When the cookies are brown, Dean takes them out. For how long do the cookies bake?

   _____

2. Dean buys carob chips for $1.29, flour for $2.50, and sugar for $3.09. How much do the sugar and flour cost?

   _____

3. Dawn sells 4 large cookies for 15¢ each and 7 small cookies for 9¢ each. How much does Dawn get for the small cookies?

   _____

4. Dean and Dawn calculate that they have sold 19 cookies. How many more large cookies than small cookies have they sold?

   _____

Mixed Applications ⟩ STRATEGIES	• Act It Out • Guess and Check • Work Backward • Find a Pattern • Write a Number Sentence

Choose a strategy and solve.

5. Dean earns $4.00, $3.59, and $3.98 in a three-day period. Are his estimated total earnings *more* than or *less* than $10.00?

   _____

6. Some cookies are arranged in a pattern of 1 large cookie, 3 small cookies. What size is the tenth cookie?

   _____

WRITER'S CORNER

7. Choose a problem above that has too little information. Add information so that it can be solved. Then find the answer.

   _____

   _____

Multiply
Using 9 as a Factor

Find the product.

1. $9 \times 3 =$ ___   2. $4 \times 9 =$ ___   3. $9 \times 1 =$ ___   4. $2 \times 9 =$ ___

5. $9 \times 7 =$ ___   6. $9 \times 9 =$ ___   7. $9 \times 5 =$ ___   8. $9 \times 8 =$ ___

9. $\begin{array}{r} 9 \\ \times 8 \\ \hline \end{array}$
10. $\begin{array}{r} 7 \\ \times 9 \\ \hline \end{array}$
11. $\begin{array}{r} 9 \\ \times 4 \\ \hline \end{array}$
12. $\begin{array}{r} 9 \\ \times 6 \\ \hline \end{array}$
13. $\begin{array}{r} 9 \\ \times 0 \\ \hline \end{array}$
14. $\begin{array}{r} 5 \\ \times 9 \\ \hline \end{array}$

15. $\begin{array}{r} 4 \\ \times 7 \\ \hline \end{array}$
16. $\begin{array}{r} 6 \\ \times 6 \\ \hline \end{array}$
17. $\begin{array}{r} 6 \\ \times 8 \\ \hline \end{array}$
18. $\begin{array}{r} 4 \\ \times 9 \\ \hline \end{array}$
19. $\begin{array}{r} 9 \\ \times 2 \\ \hline \end{array}$
20. $\begin{array}{r} 3 \\ \times 9 \\ \hline \end{array}$

Mixed Applications

Solve.

21. Mr. Eaton is 38 years old. Maria is 29 years younger than Mr. Eaton. How old is Maria?

   _____

22. A year in a human's life is said to equal 7 years in a dog's life. If a dog is 9 human-years old, what is its age in dog-years?

   _____

| NUMBER SENSE |

Fill in the numbers to make each fact true.

23. $10 \times 1 = 10$

   $9 \times 1 =$ ___ less than 10

   $10 - 1 =$ ___ , so $9 \times 1 =$ ___ .

24. $10 \times 2 = 20$

   $9 \times 2 =$ ___ less than 20

   $20 - 2 =$ ___ , so $9 \times 2 =$ ___ .

25. $10 \times 3 = 30$

   $9 \times 3 =$ ___ less than 30

   $30 - 3 =$ ___ , so $9 \times 3 =$ ___ .

26. $10 \times 4 = 40$

   $9 \times 4 =$ ___ less than 40

   $40 - 4 =$ ___ , so $9 \times 4 =$ ___ .

Three Factors

Find the product.

1. $(3 \times 2) \times 3 =$ ___

2. $2 \times (4 \times 3) =$ ___

3. $6 \times (2 \times 1) =$ ___

4. $(2 \times 4) \times 5 =$ ___

5. $3 \times (3 \times 3) =$ ___

6. $(1 \times 9) \times 6 =$ ___

7. $5 \times (3 \times 3) =$ ___

8. $(8 \times 1) \times 8 =$ ___

9. $9 \times (2 \times 4) =$ ___

Group two factors and then multiply.

10. $4 \times 2 \times 3 =$ ___

11. $7 \times 1 \times 9 =$ ___

12. $6 \times 3 \times 3 =$ ___

13. $8 \times 7 \times 1 =$ ___

14. $2 \times 3 \times 5 =$ ___

15. $3 \times 3 \times 9 =$ ___

16. $8 \times 2 \times 4 =$ ___

17. $7 \times 1 \times 7 =$ ___

18. $6 \times 1 \times 7 =$ ___

Mixed Applications

Solve.

19. Marian puts 8 teddy bears on each shelf of a toy-store display. There are 3 shelves. How many teddy bears does Marian display?

_____

20. Theo went to the toy store at 3:20. He left the store 2 hours and 30 minutes later. At what time did Theo leave the toy store?

_____

NUMBER SENSE

Choose the missing factor from the list in the box. $\boxed{8,5,3,7,6,4}$

21. $(4 \times 2) \times$ ___ $= 24$

22. ___ $\times (2 \times 3) = 30$

23. ___ $\times (1 \times 5) = 35$

24. $6 \times (1 \times$ ___ $) = 48$

25. ___ $\times (2 \times 3) = 36$

26. $(4 \times 2) \times$ ___ $= 32$

27. $(5 \times$ ___ $) \times 2 = 50$

28. $1 \times (3 \times$ ___ $) = 12$

Mental Math:
Multiplication Review

Find the product.

1. 3 ×5	2. 5 ×7	3. 8 ×9	4. 7 ×2	5. 2 ×4	6. 9 ×4
7. 8 ×3	8. 6 ×7	9. 2 ×8	10. 6 ×9	11. 8 ×5	12. 7 ×1
13. 9 ×5	14. 8 ×0	15. 5 ×7	16. 9 ×8	17. 6 ×6	18. 7 ×3

19. $4 \times 1 =$ ___   20. $8 \times 0 =$ ___   21. $1 \times 9 =$ ___   22. $4 \times 2 =$ ___

23. $0 \times 6 =$ ___   24. $1 \times 7 =$ ___   25. $3 \times 2 =$ ___   26. $3 \times 3 =$ ___

Mixed Applications

Solve.

27. Marty spent $49.95 on a radio-controlled car and $19.95 for a year's subscription to *RC Car Action* magazine. What was Marty's total cost?

_____

28. Marty spends $3 per week to race his radio-controlled car. How much does he spend for an 8-week pass to race his car?

_____

MIXED REVIEW

1. Write the value of the digit 9 in standard form.

   495,703 _____   916,407 _____   207,931 _____

2. Write the least number of coins and bills you would get as change when you give $10 for a purchase of $5.83.

_____

Problem Solving
Make Choices

Crafts Plus Prices		
Markers	**Paints**	**Clothes**
Thin — $0.69	Puffy — $1.00	Vest — $13.98
Medium — 1.05	Glitter — 1.95	Jacket — 18.00
Wide — 1.90	Neon — 2.50	Sweatshirt — 8.75

1. Wayne buys a vest. He has $3 left to spend at Crafts Plus. He wants to buy paint and a marker. What choices could he make?

   _____

   _____

2. Edie has $20 to spend on clothes, paint, and a marker at Crafts Plus. What choices could she make if she buys one of each type of item?

   _____

   _____

Mixed Applications > **STRATEGIES** • Act It Out • Guess and Check • Make a Model • Write a Number Sentence

Choose a strategy and solve.

3. Use the list above. Una buys a vest, a thin marker, and neon paint. What is the total cost?

   _____

4. Sofia buys 7 markers and 3 times as many paints. How many paints does she buy?

   _____

WRITER'S CORNER

5. Imagine that you can buy and decorate an item of clothing at Crafts Plus. Choose what you will buy and write a word problem about your purchase. Find the total cost.

   _____

Exploring Division

Manipulatives

Answer the questions for each picture.

1.

How many in

all? _____

How many

groups? _____

How many in each

group? _____

$6 \div 2 =$ _____

2.

How many in

all? _____

How many

groups? _____

How many in each

group? _____

$21 \div 3 =$ _____

3.

How many in

all? _____

How many

groups? _____

How many in each

group? _____

$12 \div 3 =$ _____

Divide. Use counters and circles.

4. $15 \div 5 =$ ___ 5. $8 \div 4 =$ ___ 6. $10 \div 2 =$ ___ 7. $28 \div 4 =$ ___

VISUAL THINKING

Complete the multiplication sentence and the
division sentence for each picture.

8.

$2 \times 2 =$ ___

$4 \div 2 =$ ___

9.

$3 \times 3 =$ ___

$9 \div 3 =$ ___

10.

$4 \times 4 =$ ___

$16 \div 4 =$ ___

Use with text pages 226–227.

Connecting Subtraction and Division

Use the pictures to solve.

1.

How many twos

are in 8? _____

8 ÷ 2 = _____

2.

How many fives

are in 15? _____

15 ÷ 5 = _____

3.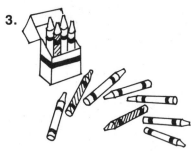

How many fours

are in 12? _____

12 ÷ 4 = _____

4. Draw 10 boxes.

Show 10 ÷ 2 = _____

5. Draw 6 chips.

Show 6 ÷ 3 = _____

6. Draw 12 sticks.

Show 12 ÷ 2 = _____

Mixed Applications

7. Ed has 8 pens. He puts them into groups of 2. Draw a picture to show how many groups of 2 pens Ed has.

8. Anna uses 1 eraser for every 2 packs of pencils she uses. If she uses 10 packs of pencils in a year, how many erasers will she use?

_____

| **WRITER'S CORNER** |

9. Write a few sentences describing one way to explain to a friend how to solve 18 ÷ 3.

_____

_____

_____

_____

Name _____

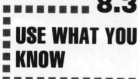
Connecting Multiplication and Division

Use the pictures to solve.

1.
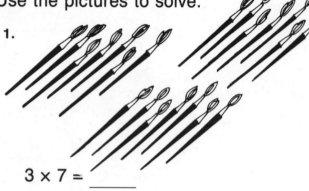

$3 \times 7 =$ _____

$21 \div 7 =$ _____

2.
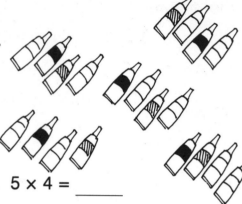

$5 \times 4 =$ _____

$20 \div 4 =$ _____

Write the fact family for each set of numbers.

3. 4, 6, 24

4. 2, 5, 10

5. 3, 9, 27

_____ _____ _____

_____ _____ _____

Mixed Applications

6. There are 18 students in Rosa's class. They are working in groups of 3. Draw a picture to show how many groups there are.

7. Some crayons are divided equally among 3 students. Each student gets 8 crayons. How many crayons are there?

_____

SCIENCE CONNECTION

Farmers in Pennsylvania have been feeding their cows chocolate to make their milk better. Each cow's daily feed includes about 4 pounds of chocolate. Tell how many cows could be fed with the following amounts of chocolate.

8. 8 pounds feeds _____ cows

9. 12 pounds feeds _____ cows

10. 24 pounds feeds _____ cows

11. 20 pounds feeds _____ cows

Use with text pages 230–231.

Dividing by 2
Using Addition Doubles

Find the quotient.

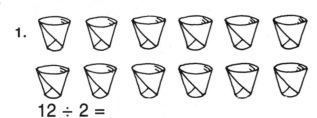

1. $12 \div 2 =$ _____

2. $10 \div 2 =$ _____

Find the missing factor.

3. $2 \times$ _____ $= 6$ 4. $2 \times$ _____ $= 10$ 5. _____ $\times 2 = 12$ 6. $9 \times$ _____ $= 18$

Find the quotient.

7. $8 \div 2 =$ _____   8. $4 \div 2 =$ _____   9. $12 \div 2 =$ _____   10. $16 \div 2 =$ _____

11. $18 \div 2 =$ _____   12. $10 \div 2 =$ _____   13. $6 \div 2 =$ _____   14. $14 \div 2 =$ _____

Mixed Applications

15. Kim earned $3 an hour for raking leaves. It took him 2 hours to do the job. How much money did he earn?

_____

16. The dividend is 12. The divisor is 2. What is the quotient?

_____

MIXED REVIEW ——————————————————

Find the product.

1. $\begin{array}{r} 8 \\ \times 3 \\ \hline \end{array}$ 2. $\begin{array}{r} 9 \\ \times 7 \\ \hline \end{array}$ 3. $\begin{array}{r} 3 \\ \times 8 \\ \hline \end{array}$ 4. $\begin{array}{r} 5 \\ \times 9 \\ \hline \end{array}$ 5. $\begin{array}{r} 7 \\ \times 8 \\ \hline \end{array}$ 6. $\begin{array}{r} 4 \\ \times 6 \\ \hline \end{array}$

Write the money amount.

7.

_____

8.

_____

Problem Solving
Choose a Strategy

Mixed Applications >	STRATEGIES	• Act It Out • Guess and Check • Draw a Picture • Write a Number Sentence

Choose a strategy and solve.

1. Carmen practices piano for 5 minutes a day. For how many minutes does she practice in a 6-day period?

_____

2. Mrs. Lopez, Carrie's piano teacher, teaches 3 classes a day, 5 days a week. How many classes does she teach in 5 days?

_____

3. Greg practices piano for 20 minutes a day. He plays each piece he is assigned for 5 minutes. How many pieces does he practice each day?

_____

4. Mrs. Lopez receives 12 roses from a student. She divides them equally among 4 vases. How many roses are in each vase?

_____

5. The piano recital is 4 weeks from today. In how many days is the recital?

_____

6. Tickets for the recital cost $6 for adults and $4 for children. How much will it cost for 2 adults and 3 children to go to the recital?

_____

MUSIC CONNECTION

A *duet* is a song played or sung by two musicians.
Tell the number of duets a class could play if there were

7. 6 students. _____

8. 10 students _____

9. 14 students. _____

10. 18 students _____

Use with text pages 234–235.

Name _____

Dividing by 3

Write a division sentence for each.

1.

_____

2.

_____

Find the quotient.

3. $12 \div 3 =$ ____   4. $18 \div 3 =$ ____   5. $21 \div 3 =$ ____   6. $8 \div 2 =$ ____

7. $18 \div 2 =$ ____   8. $24 \div 3 =$ ____   9. $9 \div 3 =$ ____   10. $6 \div 3 =$ ____

Write × or ÷ for ◯ .

11. $15 \bigcirc 3 = 5$ 12. $4 \bigcirc 2 = 8$ 13. $9 \bigcirc 3 = 3$ 14. $3 \bigcirc 7 = 21$

Mixed Applications

15. The checkers tournament began at 11:30. It ended 2 hours and 30 minutes later. At what time was it over?

_____

16. At the party after the tournament, Tom spent $0.65 for lemonade, $1.25 for a hot dog, and $0.95 for an apple. How much did Tom spend?

_____

| **VISUAL THINKING** |

17. Connect the dots with 6 lines to make 2 squares. How many corners do the 2 squares have?

_____

18. Draw 3 more lines to make 6 triangles. How many corners do the 6 triangles have?

_____

Dividing by 4

Find the quotient.

1. 24 ÷ 4 = ____   2. 15 ÷ 3 = ____   3. 12 ÷ 2 = ____   4. 16 ÷ 4 = ____

5. 28 ÷ 4 = ____   6. 12 ÷ 4 = ____   7. 20 ÷ 4 = ____   8. 27 ÷ 3 = ____

9. 24 ÷ 3 = ____   10. 24 ÷ 4 = ____   11. 32 ÷ 4 = ____   12. 36 ÷ 4 = ____

13. 4)12   14. 4)8   15. 3)9   16. 2)16   17. 4)24   18. 3)15

19. 3)21   20. 4)20   21. 4)28   22. 2)18   23. 4)32   24. 4)36

Mixed Applications

25. The third-grade class used rhythm instruments in their show. Twenty four students shared 6 instruments. How many students shared each instrument?

26. The class sang 8 songs. Each song lasted about 2 minutes. How many minutes did all of the songs take?

_____

NUMBER SENSE

Study the tables. Then write *more* or *fewer* to complete each sentence.

Number of Toys for Each Child

Toys	3 Children	4 Children	6 Children
24	8	6	4

Number of Acorns for Each Squirrel

Squirrels	16 Acorns	12 Acorns	8 Acorns
4	4	3	2

27. If the number of toys stays the same, then the more children there are the _____ toys each child gets.

28. If the number of squirrels stays the same, then the _____ acorns there are the fewer acorns each squirrel gets.

Dividing by 5

Find the quotient.

1. $5\overline{)15}$ 2. $4\overline{)16}$ 3. $5\overline{)10}$ 4. $2\overline{)12}$ 5. $5\overline{)25}$ 6. $4\overline{)12}$

7. $5\overline{)20}$ 8. $2\overline{)10}$ 9. $5\overline{)30}$ 10. $3\overline{)18}$ 11. $4\overline{)28}$ 12. $5\overline{)45}$

13. $5\overline{)35}$ 14. $4\overline{)24}$ 15. $3\overline{)21}$ 16. $5\overline{)40}$ 17. $3\overline{)15}$ 18. $4\overline{)20}$

19. $25 \div 5 =$ ___   20. $40 \div 5 =$ ___   21. $24 \div 4 =$ ___   22. $18 \div 3 =$ ___

23. $45 \div 5 =$ ___   24. $5 \div 5 =$ ___   25. $16 \div 4 =$ ___   26. $8 \div 2 =$ ___

Mixed Applications

27. Sarina made 8 bracelets out of yarn. She used 5 strands of yarn for each bracelet. How many strands of yarn did Sarina use?

    _____

28. A skein of yarn is 15 feet long. Sarina needs 3 feet to make a necklace. How many necklaces can Sarina make from one skein?

    _____

EVERYDAY MATH CONNECTION

Liza works at an arcade. She trades quarters for nickels so that customers can play the arcade games.

29. Quint has 10 nickels. How many quarters will Liza give Quint?

    _____

30. Cai has 25 nickels. How many quarters will Liza give Cai?

    _____

31. Liza gives Pat 3 quarters. How many nickels did Pat give to Liza?

    _____

32. Wes gives Liza some nickels. She gives Wes 8 quarters. How many nickels did Wes give Liza?

    _____

Name _____

Dividing Using 0 and 1

Find the quotient.

1. $2 \div 2 =$ ___
2. $0 \div 2 =$ ___
3. $7 \div 1 =$ ___
4. $20 \div 4 =$ ___

5. $8 \div 1 =$ ___
6. $0 \div 5 =$ ___
7. $9 \div 9 =$ ___
8. $0 \div 4 =$ ___

9. $0 \div 6 =$ ___
10. $12 \div 3 =$ ___
11. $5 \div 1 =$ ___
12. $3 \div 3 =$ ___

13. $6 \div 1 =$ ___
14. $8 \div 8 =$ ___
15. $27 \div 3 =$ ___
16. $7 \div 7 =$ ___

Mixed Applications

Write a number sentence and solve.

17. Luis spent 1 hour molding a clay bowl. Then it took him 25 minutes to glaze the bowl. How much longer did Luis spend molding the bowl?

18. There were 8 different glaze colors to choose from. The art teacher had 4 jars of each color. How many jars did the art teacher have?

19. The art teacher placed 87 clay bowls and 18 clay vases in the kiln to be fired. How many pieces were being fired in the kiln?

20. Clay is shipped in 36-pound blocks. Each block is divided equally into 9 smaller blocks. How many pounds does each smaller block weigh?

NUMBER SENSE

Complete.

21. $7 \times 4 = 28$, so $28 \div$ ___ $= 7$.
22. $9 \times 3 = 27$, so $27 \div$ ___ $= 9$.

23. $8 \times 5 = 40$, so $40 \div$ ___ $= 8$.
24. $6 \times 4 = 24$, so $24 \div$ ___ $= 6$.

25. $36 \div 4 = 9$, so $9 \times$ ___ $= 36$.
26. $21 \div 3 = 7$, so $7 \times$ ___ $= 21$.

Use with text pages 244–245.

Problem Solving
Multistep Problems

1. Jack bought paints for $2.98 and brushes for $1.75. How much change did he receive from a $5 bill?

   _____

2. Jack paints 6 model cars with each large jar of paint, and 3 cars with each small jar. He buys 2 large jars and 1 small jar. How many cars can he paint?

   _____

3. Jack sells painted model cars for $8.98. Unpainted cars cost $5.49. Jack sells 2 painted cars and 2 unpainted cars. How much does he get?

   _____

4. A toy store sells 358 model trucks, 247 model cars, and 315 model airplanes. How many more models must it sell to total 1,000?

   _____

Mixed Applications	STRATEGIES	• Work Backward • Draw a Picture • Write a Number Sentence

Choose a strategy and solve.

5. Jack paints 4 cars red, 3 cars blue, and 7 cars white. He paints the rest of the 25 cars black. How many are black?

   _____

6. A jar of regular paint costs $1.98. Neon paint costs $0.75 more than regular paint. How much does neon paint cost?

   _____

MIXED REVIEW

1. Ring the numbers that would round to 600.

   597   613   624   555   651   704   580   648

Find the sum or difference.

2.	3.	4.	5.	6.
802	345	980	$8.97	$6.00
− 186	+ 755	− 893	+ 1.59	− 2.79

Mental Math:
Reviewing Facts

Draw a picture for each division sentence. Solve.

1. 16 ÷ 4 = _____

2. 10 ÷ 5 = _____

3. 5 ÷ 5 = _____

Find the quotient.

4. 18 ÷ 3 = _____

5. 24 ÷ 4 = _____

6. 25 ÷ 5 = _____

7. 21 ÷ 3 = _____

8. 15 ÷ 5 = _____

9. 14 ÷ 2 = _____

10. 12 ÷ 4 = _____

11. 20 ÷ 4 = _____

12. $5\overline{)30}$

13. $4\overline{)28}$

14. $2\overline{)8}$

15. $3\overline{)24}$

16. $5\overline{)40}$

17. $1\overline{)8}$

18. $3\overline{)12}$

19. $5\overline{)5}$

20. $3\overline{)9}$

21. $4\overline{)36}$

22. $5\overline{)20}$

23. $2\overline{)18}$

Mixed Applications

24. A fire was reported to the fire station at 2:35. The fire trucks got to the fire 12 minutes later. What time was it then?

_____

25. Hillside Fire Station has 36 workers. They are grouped into 9 teams. How many workers are in each team?

_____

VISUAL THINKING

Write two division sentences for each picture.

26.

_____

_____

27.

_____

_____

28.

_____

_____

Use with text pages 256–257.

Division with a Multiplication Table

Use the multiplication table. Find the missing factor.

1. $5 \times$ _____ $= 20$ 2. _____ $\times 6 = 24$

×	2	3	4	5	6
2	4	6	8	10	12
3	6	9	12	15	18
4	8	12	16	20	24
5	10	15	20	25	30
6	12	18	24	30	36

3. $2 \times$ _____ $= 10$ 4. _____ $\times 3 = 9$

Use the table to find the quotient.

5. $16 \div 4 =$ _____   6. $30 \div 5 =$ _____   7. $8 \div 2 =$ _____   8. $36 \div 6 =$ _____

9. $25 \div 5 =$ _____   10. $12 \div 4 =$ _____   11. $18 \div 6 =$ _____   12. $24 \div 6 =$ _____

13. $5\overline{)20}$ 14. $2\overline{)6}$ 15. $3\overline{)18}$ 16. $4\overline{)24}$ 17. $5\overline{)15}$ 18. $6\overline{)30}$ 19. $3\overline{)12}$

Mixed Applications

20. A train carries food to several grocery stores. There are 885 cartons of canned goods, 802 cartons of eggs, and 840 cartons of vegetables. Order the cartons from least to greatest.

_____

21. The clerks at Ed's Grocery Store stack the vegetable cartons in the back of the store. They stack 4 rows of cartons. Each row is stacked 8 cartons high. How many vegetable cartons are there?

_____

MIXED REVIEW

Write the numbers in standard form.

1. fourteen thousand, three hundred seventy-nine _____

2. three hundred two thousand, eight hundred sixty _____

Write a multiplication and a division fact family for the set of numbers.

3. 4, 3, 12 _____

Dividing by 6

Find the quotient.

1. $18 \div 6 = $ ___   2. $54 \div 6 = $ ___   3. $0 \div 6 = $ ___   4. $12 \div 6 = $ ___

5. $20 \div 5 = $ ___   6. $36 \div 6 = $ ___   7. $45 \div 5 = $ ___   8. $42 \div 6 = $ ___

9. $48 \div 6 = $ ___   10. $0 \div 6 = $ ___   11. $30 \div 6 = $ ___   12. $28 \div 4 = $ ___

13. $6\overline{)24}$ 14. $6\overline{)6}$ 15. $6\overline{)18}$ 16. $6\overline{)30}$ 17. $6\overline{)54}$ 18. $6\overline{)0}$

19. $6\overline{)12}$ 20. $5\overline{)40}$ 21. $2\overline{)18}$ 22. $6\overline{)48}$ 23. $4\overline{)24}$ 24. $6\overline{)36}$

25. $5\overline{)30}$ 26. $4\overline{)28}$ 27. $3\overline{)24}$ 28. $2\overline{)16}$ 29. $3\overline{)21}$ 30. $5\overline{)35}$

Mixed Applications

31. The quotient is 3 more than the divisor. The dividend is 18. What are the quotient and the divisor?

_____

32. Patti's Pet Store has 24 kittens. They are kept in 6 cages. How many kittens are in each cage?

_____

LOGICAL REASONING

Marnie works in the office of a garden-supplies store. She needs to buy 6 pencils for use in the office. She has two choices.

a. pencils that are sold 6 to a box and cost $0.36 a box

b. pencils that are sold separately and cost $0.08 each

33. To spend the least amount of money, should she choose **a** or **b**? How much money will she save by buying the less expensive pencils?

Use with text pages 260–261.

Problem Solving
Choose the Operation

1. Terri schedules patients for Dr. Cruz to treat. She schedules 4 patients for a 1-hour period. Dr. Cruz works 7 hours a day. How many patients does Terri schedule for Dr. Cruz to see in a day?

_____ _____

2. Dr. Cruz works in a medical building. Altogether, 24 doctors work in the building. The building has 8 office spaces. An equal number of doctors use each office space. How many doctors work in each office space?

_____

3. There are 6 doctors who share one large office in a medical building. Each doctor has 3 nurses who help with daily jobs. How many nurses work in the large office?

_____

4. Joseph is now 51 inches tall. The doctor told Joseph that he had grown 5 inches since the last checkup. How tall was Joseph then?

_____

Mixed Applications ⟩	**STRATEGIES**	• Act It Out • Guess and Check • Work Backward • Find a Pattern

Choose a strategy and solve.   **Choices of strategies may vary.**

5. There are 4 children in the doctor's waiting room. Meg will be seen after Jo. Bee will be seen before Juan. Jo will be seen first. Meg will be seen before Bee. In what order will the children be seen?

_____

6. Dr. Malone bought some new books for her office waiting room. For every 3 children's books she bought, she received 1 book for parents at no cost. If there were 16 books in the shipment, how many free parents' books did Dr. Malone receive?

_____

Dividing by 7

Find the quotient.

1. $14 \div 7 =$ ____   2. $28 \div 7 =$ ____   3. $7 \div 7 =$ ____   4. $49 \div 7 =$ ____

5. $42 \div 7 =$ ____   6. $21 \div 7 =$ ____   7. $63 \div 7 =$ ____   8. $56 \div 7 =$ ____

9. $7\overline{)35}$ 10. $7\overline{)14}$ 11. $6\overline{)42}$ 12. $7\overline{)28}$ 13. $3\overline{)27}$ 14. $7\overline{)56}$

15. $7\overline{)21}$ 16. $6\overline{)36}$ 17. $4\overline{)0}$ 18. $6\overline{)24}$ 19. $7\overline{)63}$ 20. $7\overline{)7}$

Write × or ÷ in each ◯

21. $7 \bigcirc 9 = 63$ 22. $42 \bigcirc 7 = 6$ 23. $36 \bigcirc 6 = 6$ 24. $8 \bigcirc 2 = 4$

Mixed Applications

25. Julio works at a plant nursery. He waters 1,234 flower plants, 217 bushes, and 48 trees. How many plants does Julio water in all?

_____

26. Mr. Chu buys 9 mum plants. After careful rooting and replanting of these mums, Mr. Chu has 63 mums two years later. If an equal number came from each of the original mums, how many mums did he grow from each original plant?

_____

SCIENCE CONNECTION

A plant gets water through its roots. Then the water moves up the stem to the leaves. In an experiment, a celery stalk was placed in red-colored water. Every hour, the red water traveled another 3 cm up the stalk.

27. How many hours did it take for the red water to travel 12 cm up the celery stalk?

_____

28. If the stalk is 21 cm long, how many hours will it take for the water to travel from one end of the stalk to the other?

_____

       Use with text pages 266–267.

Dividing by 8

Find the missing factor.

1. $4 \times$ ____ $= 32$ 2. $5 \times$ ____ $= 0$ 3. ____ $\times 9 = 63$ 4. $8 \times$ ____ $= 48$

Find the quotient.

5. $7 \times 8 = 56$, so $56 \div 8 =$ ____ .

6. $3 \times 8 = 24$, so $24 \div 8 =$ ____ .

7. $5 \times 8 = 40$, so $40 \div 8 =$ ____ .

8. $9 \times 8 = 72$, so $72 \div 8 =$ ____ .

9. $2 \times 8 = 16$, so $16 \div 8 =$ ____ .

10. $0 \times 8 = 0$, so $0 \div 8 =$ ____ .

11. $8\overline{)24}$ 12. $6\overline{)24}$ 13. $5\overline{)40}$ 14. $7\overline{)42}$ 15. $8\overline{)56}$ 16. $5\overline{)5}$

17. $4\overline{)36}$ 18. $8\overline{)48}$ 19. $4\overline{)32}$ 20. $5\overline{)45}$ 21. $8\overline{)72}$ 22. $8\overline{)64}$

Mixed Applications

23. Ms. West's third grade is having a mathathon. Each student is asked to complete a 72-problem booklet in 8 days. Millie will do the same number of problems each day. How many problems will she do each day?

_____

24. Millie sees that 3 pages in the math booklet each have 9 addition problems, and 4 pages each have 7 subtraction problems. Are there more addition or more subtraction problems in the booklet?

_____

MIXED REVIEW

Find the sum or difference.

1. $\begin{array}{r} 8,345 \\ 2,468 \\ 42 \\ +\ 846 \\ \hline \end{array}$

2. $\begin{array}{r} 3,901 \\ 1,023 \\ 9 \\ +2,497 \\ \hline \end{array}$

3. $\begin{array}{r} 809 \\ -\ 397 \\ \hline \end{array}$

4. $\begin{array}{r} \$89.26 \\ 12.09 \\ +\ \ 7.95 \\ \hline \end{array}$

5. $\begin{array}{r} \$4.00 \\ -\ 1.56 \\ \hline \end{array}$

Dividing by 9

Find the quotient.

1. 54 ÷ 9 = ____   2. 36 ÷ 9 = ____   3. 81 ÷ 9 = ____   4. 27 ÷ 3 = ____

5. 18 ÷ 9 = ____   6. 72 ÷ 8 = ____   7. 48 ÷ 6 = ____   8. 21 ÷ 7 = ____

9. 9)36   10. 7)42   11. 9)81   12. 7)63   13. 9)9   14. 7)56

15. 8)48   16. 9)45   17. 9)0   18. 9)63   19. 6)54   20. 9)27

Mixed Applications

21. The Springdale Sports Club has 63 students signed up for baseball teams. There are 7 equal-size teams formed. How many students are on each team?

_____

22. One baseball team collects $5 from each of its 9 players to buy the coach a gift. How much money is collected?

_____

23. One factor is 2 less than the other. The product is 48. What are the factors?

_____

24. In one game, Kristi scores 4 more runs than Jon. Jon scores 1 run fewer than Carlos. Carlos scores 3 runs. How many runs do Jon and Kristi each score?

_____

| **WRITER'S CORNER** |

25. Write a problem that you can solve by dividing by 9.

_____
_____
_____
_____

Exploring Dividing with Remainders

Draw a picture to show each division problem.
Use counters to help you.

1. $3\overline{)17}$ 2. $4\overline{)9}$ 3. $5\overline{)23}$

Write each division problem the other way.

4. $15 \div 4 =$ _____   5. $37 \div 6 =$ _____   6. $18 \div 7 =$ _____

Find the quotient. Use counters to help you.

7. $2\overline{)15}$ 8. $3\overline{)16}$ 9. $6\overline{)14}$ 10. $4\overline{)38}$ 11. $7\overline{)11}$

12. $3\overline{)25}$ 13. $6\overline{)15}$ 14. $7\overline{)23}$ 15. $5\overline{)29}$ 16. $2\overline{)17}$

17. $5\overline{)18}$ 18. $9\overline{)20}$ 19. $8\overline{)12}$ 20. $6\overline{)34}$ 21. $7\overline{)29}$

EVERYDAY MATH CONNECTION

Betsy and her friends play a card game with 25 cards. The cards are divided evenly among the players. For each number of players below, how many cards are there per player, and how many cards are left over?

22. 3 players _____

23. 6 players _____

24. 4 players _____

Problem Solving
Choose the Method

Write **a, b, c,** or **d** to tell which method you would
use to solve each problem. Then solve.
- **a.** objects
- **b.** paper and pencil
- **c.** calculator
- **d.** mental math

1. Bloomington School's office has 4 telephone lines. About 6 calls an hour come in on each line. About how many calls does the school get in 1 hour?

_____

2. Camden schools have 21,356 elementary school students and 27,520 junior high and high school students. How many students go to Camden schools?

_____

3. School begins at 8:30. Lunch is served 3 hours and 15 minutes later. At what time is lunch served?

_____

4. Sue is first in the lunch line. Jeff is behind Stan. Stan is between Jeff and Sue. In what order are the students in line?

_____

Mixed Applications ⟩ **STRATEGIES** • Guess and Check • Work Backward
• Make a Model • Write a Number Sentence

Choose a strategy and solve.

5. The math period for Mr. Okada's class ends at 1:45. The period lasts 1 hour. At what time does the math period begin?

_____

6. Jennifer is reading a book that has 217 pages. She has 48 pages left to read. How many pages has Jennifer read?

_____

NUMBER SENSE _____

Continue the pattern.

7. 7, 14, 21, _____, _____, _____

8. 54, 48, 42, _____, _____, _____

9. 4, 12, 20, _____, _____, _____

10. 5, 15, 25, _____, _____, _____

Use with text pages 274–275.

Name _____

Exploring Solid Figures
Manipulatives

   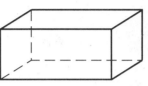

| Cube | Cone | Cylinder | Sphere | Rectangular Prism | Pyramid |

Name the figure that each looks like.

1.

_____

2.

_____

3.

_____

4.

_____

5.

_____

6.

_____

Solve the riddle. Use your solid figures.

7. I have 5 faces. All but 1 are triangles. What am I?

_____

8. I have 6 faces. Only 2 are squares. What am I?

_____

| **WRITER'S CORNER** |

9. Write a riddle that has a solid figure as its answer.

_____

_____

_____

_____

_____

Exploring Plane Figures

Name the figure that each looks like.

1.
_____

2.
_____

3.
_____

4.
_____

5.
_____

6.
_____

Draw a line from the description to the figure.

7. 4 sides and 4 corners
   All sides are the same length.

8. 4 sides and 4 corners
   All sides are not the same length.

9. 3 sides and 3 corners

10. 0 sides and 0 corners

11. 5 sides and 5 corners

rectangle

circle

pentagon

square

triangle

EVERYDAY MATH CONNECTION

Name two things in the kitchen of your home that are shaped like each figure listed.

12. Square   _____   _____

13. Rectangle   _____   _____

14. Circle   _____   _____

Use with text pages 286–287.

Exploring Line Segments and Angles

Find the number of line segments in each figure.

1.

2.

3.

_____   _____   _____

Write whether each angle is a *right angle* or *less than* or *greater than* a right angle.

4.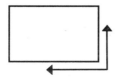

5.

6.

_____   _____   _____

Draw each figure.

7. I have 4 right angles.
I have 4 sides. All are
the same length.

8. I have 0 right angles.
I have 6 sides.
I have 6 angles.

EVERYDAY MATH CONNECTION

Each kind of road sign has a special shape. Write the word or words that might be written inside each sign.

9.

10.

11.

_____   _____   _____

Name _____

Exploring Congruent Figures

Tell whether the two figures are congruent.
Write *yes* or *no.*

1.

2.

3.

_____   _____   _____

Ring the figure that is congruent to the shaded
figure.

4.

5.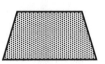

6.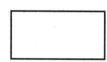

7. Write a sentence describing how you can tell
whether two figures are congruent.

_____

_____

| MIXED REVIEW |

Solve.

1. $3 \times 5 =$ ___   2. $4 \times 8 =$ ___   3. $36 \div 9 =$ ___   4. $72 \div 8 =$ ___

Find the quotient. Use counters to help you.

5. $3\overline{)13}$ 6. $4\overline{)18}$ 7. $5\overline{)12}$ 8. $2\overline{)15}$ 9. $6\overline{)9}$

Use with text pages 290–291.

Name _____

Exploring Symmetry

Trace the figure. Cut out your drawing and fold it in
half. Write *yes* or *no* to tell whether the figure has a
line of symmetry.

1.

2.

3.

_____   _____   _____

Is the dotted line a line of symmetry? Write *yes* or *no.*

4.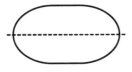

5.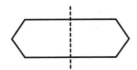

6.

_____   _____   _____

● Draw a line of symmetry.

7.

8.

9.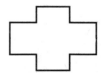

┌─────────────────────┐
│ **VISUAL THINKING** │─────────────────────────
└─────────────────────┘

10. Draw an open figure.   11. Draw a closed figure.

Name _____

Problem-Solving Strategy
Find a Pattern

1. Diego's schedule for practicing piano follows a pattern. He practices for 5 minutes on Monday, 8 minutes on Tuesday, 11 minutes on Wednesday, and 14 minutes on Thursday. For how many minutes does Diego practice on Friday? on Saturday?

   _____

   _____

2. Megan is saving her pennies for a new piano book. She saves 1 penny the first day. On the second day she saves 2 pennies, on the third day she saves 4 pennies, and on the fourth day she saves 8 pennies. How many pennies will she save on the fifth day? on the sixth day?

   _____

   _____

Mixed Applications > **STRATEGIES** • Guess and Check • Find a Pattern • Write a Number Sentence • Draw a Picture

Choose a strategy and solve.

3. It is 4:00 when Ned and Sue begin a math project. Ned finishes it in 15 minutes. Sue finishes 8 minutes later than Ned. At what time does Sue finish the math project?

   _____

4. Zack and Jack play a pattern game. Zack says 4, and Jack says 8. Zack says 5, and Jack says 10. Zack says 6, and Jack says 12. What does Jack say when Zack says 7? What does Jack say when Zack says 9?

   _____

VISUAL THINKING _____

5. Draw the two shapes that will come next.

Use with text pages 294–295.

Exploring Perimeter

Choose a book from your desk, classroom, or home.
Find its perimeter three times. Each time use a
different unit of measure. Use the units of measure in
the list below.

    a. width of your finger
    b. width of a pencil
    c. width of a paper clip

Complete the table.

	Unit of Measure	Guess	Perimeter
1.	Finger width		
2.	Pencil width		
3.	Clip width		

Use the width of a crayon. Find the perimeter of
each figure.

4. _____ units

5. 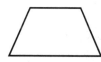 _____ units

6. _____ units

7. _____ units

CAREER CONNECTION

James is a carpenter. He is putting wood trim around
the window in a hallway. He needs to know the
perimeter of the window so that he can buy the
correct amount of wood.

8. Write a sentence describing how James could
use a ruler to find the perimeter.

_____

_____

Name _____

Exploring Area

Fill in squares with your pencil. Make three shapes, each with an area of 6 square units.

1.

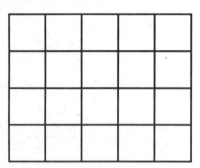

2.

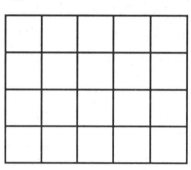

3.

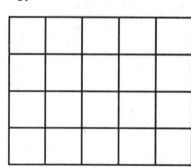

Find the area of each figure. Label your answer in square units.

4.

_____

5.

_____

6.

_____

7.

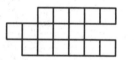

_____

8.

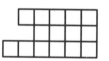

_____

9.

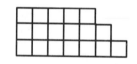

_____

VISUAL THINKING

The area of this figure is 4 square units.
Write the area of each figure below.

10.

_____

11.

_____

12.

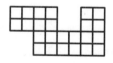

_____

13. Write a sentence telling how you found your answers.

_____

_____

Use with text pages 300–301.

Exploring Volume

Manipulatives

Use cubes to build the shapes. Find the volume of
each shape.

1.

_____

2.

_____

3.
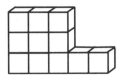

_____

4.
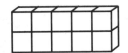

_____

5.
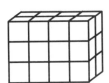

_____

6.
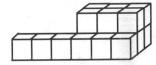

_____

7.
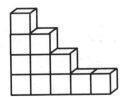

_____

8.

_____

9.
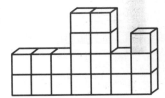

_____

MIXED REVIEW

Find the sum or difference.

1.	2.	3.	4.	5.
457	689	4,109	$3.09	$16.75
+398	−297	+2,863	− 1.98	+ 4.50

Write × or ÷ for ◯ .

6. 8 ◯ 5 = 40   7. 72 ◯ 9 = 8   8. 45 ◯ 5 = 9   9. 6 ◯ 6 = 36

Name _____

Using Points on a Grid

Write the ordered pair for each letter.

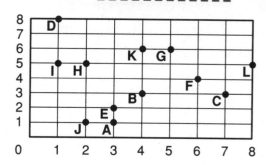

1. A
____

2. B
____

3. F
____

4. H
____

5. G
____

6. I
____

7. K
____

8. L
____

Name the letter for each ordered pair.

9. (3,2) ____   10. (7,3) ____   11. (2,1) ____   12. (1,8) ____

Mixed Applications

13. Use the grid at the top of the page. If the letter E is moved to the right 2 spaces and up 1 space, what word would you see?

_____

14. Yoshi's family has an egg farm. Yoshi and his 2 sisters each gathered 6 eggs one day. How many eggs did they gather in all?

_____

15. Gretel bought a carton of eggs for $1.17. She gave the clerk $2.00. How much change did she receive?

_____

16. Gretel's mother was making cakes for the bake sale. She needed 3 eggs for each cake. How many cakes could she make with 24 eggs?

_____

EVERYDAY MATH CONNECTION

Imagine the grid at the right is a map. Tell the location of these places.

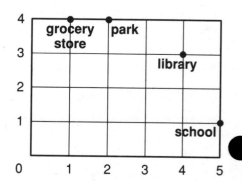

17. library _____   18. grocery store _____

19. school _____   20. park _____

Use with text pages 304–305.

Problem-Solving Strategy
Make a Pictograph

Number of Circus Tickets Sold

Monday	🎫🎫🎫🎫🎫🎫
Tuesday	🎫🎫🎫🎫🎫
Wednesday	🎫🎫🎫🎫
Thursday	🎫🎫🎫🎫🎫🎫
Friday	🎫🎫🎫🎫🎫🎫🎫🎫
Saturday	🎫🎫🎫🎫🎫🎫🎫

Each 🎫 = 5 tickets

1. On which day were the fewest tickets sold?

   _____

2. How many more tickets were sold on Friday than on Thursday?

   _____

3. Make a pictograph of lunch choices for a third-grade class. There are 16 students who bring lunch, 8 students who buy hot lunch, and 12 students who buy cold lunch. Use ☺ to show students. Have 1 ☺ stand for 2 students.

1 ☺ = 2 students

4. Write the title on the line above your graph.

Mixed Applications

5. In the pictograph above, Ernesto wants to make 1 ☺ stand for 4 students. How many ☺'s would he draw for bringing lunch?

   _____

6. The school sold 425 hot lunches on Monday. It sold 87 fewer hot lunches on Tuesday. How many hot lunches did it sell on Tuesday?

   _____

NUMBER SENSE

7. Suppose a pictograph is to show classes of 35, 40, 20, 45, and 30 students. How many students would you have each symbol stand for? Explain.

   _____

Exploring Length
Inch

Manipulatives

Measure the length of each in inches.

1.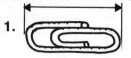

2.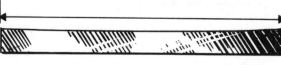

3.

Draw each length from the •.

4. 2 inches •

5. 1 inch •

6. 4 inches •

7. Find two things in your desk or classroom that measure about 9 inches each.

_____

Mixed Applications

8. Marcy's ribbon is 12 inches long. She cuts a 9-inch piece to tie into a bow. How much ribbon is left?

9. Jorge connects 2-inch paper clips to make a chain. How long is Jorge's chain if he uses 5 paper clips?

LOGICAL REASONING

10. Yoshi glues his report to a piece of colored paper. The report paper is 8 inches wide and 10 inches long. The colored paper makes a 1-inch border around the report paper. How wide is the colored paper?

Use with text pages 316–317.

Length
Foot, Yard, and Mile

Ring the better estimate.

1. the length of a piece of paper

   11 inches or 11 feet

2. the length of a football field

   100 feet or 100 yards

3. the length of your classroom

   20 yards or 20 miles

4. the distance from your home to school

   2 yards or 2 miles

5. the height of your chair

   2 feet or 2 yards

6. the distance a car travels

   20 yards or 20 miles

Mixed Applications

7. Jeremiah buys tomato plants for his garden. He spaces them 18 inches apart. How many inches from the first plant is the third plant? Draw a picture.

   _____

8. Jeremiah's garden is a rectangle that measures 2 feet long and 6 feet wide. What is the perimeter of the garden?

   _____

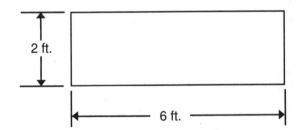

2 ft.

6 ft.

SCIENCE CONNECTION

9. A potato plant grows to a height of 4 inches within two weeks of planting. It then grows another inch every 3 days. In how many days from planting will the potato plant be 10 inches tall?

   _____

Name _____

Exploring Capacity
Customary Units

Ring the better estimate.

1. 1 quart or 1 gallon

2. 1 pint or 1 gallon

3. 5 pints or 5 gallons

4. 1 cup or 1 quart

Tell which unit of measure you would use. Write *c*, *pt*, *qt*, or *gal*.

5. milk in a glass

   about 1 _____

6. water in an aquarium

   about 10 _____

7. water in a cooler

   about 4 _____

8. juice in a small carton

   about 1 _____

Complete the table.

9.

Cups	4	8	12	16	20	24
Pints	2		6	8		12
Quarts	1	2			5	

Ring the greater amount.

10. 2 pints or 2 quarts

11. 8 cups or 2 pints

12. 4 pints or 1 quart

13. 4 cups or 2 quarts

NUMBER SENSE

14. Pepita is making punch for the school party. She wants 1 pint of sherbet for every 2 quarts of juice. Pepita has 2 gallon jugs of apple juice and 2 quart cartons of cranberry juice. How many pints of sherbet does Pepita need?

   _____

Use with text pages 320–321.

Exploring Weight
Ounce and Pound

Which unit of measure would you use to weigh each item? Write *ounce* or *pound*.

1. _____

2.  _____

3.  _____

4.  _____

Ring the better estimate.

5. 1 pound
   or
   1 ounce

6. 8 ounces
   or
   8 pounds

7. 25 ounces
   or
   25 pounds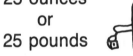

8. 10 ounces
   or
   10 pounds

Solve.

9. A can with 3 tennis balls weighs 14 ounces. Do the tennis balls weigh *more than* or *less than* 1 pound?

_____

10. Su-Lyn wears 2 wrist weights that weigh 12 ounces each. What is the total weight of the wrist weights?

_____

MIXED REVIEW

Find the product or quotient.

1. $4 \times 9 =$ ___
2. $72 \div 8 =$ ___
3. $8 \times 7 =$ ___
4. $14 \div 7 =$ ___

5. $7\overline{)63}$
6. $9\overline{)72}$
7. $3\overline{)24}$
8. $5\overline{)40}$
9. $9\overline{)18}$
10. $6\overline{)6}$

Name _____

Exploring Fahrenheit Temperature

Ring the more reasonable temperature.

1. hot soup

    50°F or 120°F

2. sledding party

    30°F or 80°F

3. swimming party

    15°F or 85°F

Write each temperature.

4.

5.

6.

7.

_____   _____   _____   _____

Mixed Applications

Solve.

8. When Ruth woke up, the thermometer read 45°F. Two hours later the temperature had risen 17°. What was the temperature then?

    _____

9. A fan will go on if the temperature goes above room temperature. Will the fan go on if the thermometer reads 50°F?

    _____

EVERYDAY MATH CONNECTION

Draw a line to match the temperature on each thermometer to the right clothes that should be worn.

10.

11.

12.

13.

Use with text pages 324–325.

Name _____

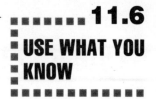
Problem Solving
Choose a Strategy

| Mixed Applications > | STRATEGIES | • Write a Number Sentence • Act It Out • Draw a Picture • Guess and Check |

Choose a strategy and solve.

1. Keith is swimming in the middle lane of the pool. He waves to Juan, who is 3 lanes away, in the end lane. How many lanes does the pool have?

_____

2. Lian has 36-inch shoelaces. After lacing her shoes, she finds that there are 10 inches on each end for tying. How many inches are used to lace the shoes?

_____

3. Members of the swim team lined up in order from shortest to tallest. There were 6 people behind Paula. There were 13 swimmers in all. How many people were in front of Paula?

4. Paula bought a team swimsuit for $22.75, a swim cap for $5.50, and goggles for $4.95. She also spent $15.00 on team membership. What was Paula's total cost to join the swim team?

LOGICAL REASONING

5. There are 8 people in a line. Maria is at the front of the line. There are 3 people between Maria and Jeff. Max is behind Jeff. There is one person between Max and Jeff. What is Max's position in line?

_____

Name _____

Exploring Length
Centimeter

Manipulatives

Measure the length of each in centimeters.

1.

2.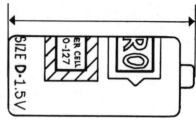

_____   _____

Draw each length from the •.

3. 2 centimeters •

4. 3 centimeters •

5. 12 centimeters •

Solve.

6. When Sofia tapped the golf ball, it moved 35 centimeters. It is still 17 centimeters from the hole. How far was the ball from the hole before Sofia tapped it?

7. The yellow golf ball is 16 centimeters from the hole. The red golf ball is 7 centimeters closer. How far is the red golf ball from the hole?

_____   _____

LOGICAL REASONING

A crayon measures about 8 centimeters. A crayon can be used to estimate lengths of other objects. Measure the objects using an 8-centimeter crayon. Then multiply by 8 to find the approximate length.

	crayons	centimeters
8. the length of your math book	_____	_____
9. the length of a pencil	_____	_____
10. the height of your chair	_____	_____

Use with text pages 330–331.

Exploring Length
Meter and Kilometer

Ring the better estimate.

1. the length of a chalkboard

   8 meters or 80 meters

2. the height of a child

   1 meter or 5 meters

Is it *more* than or *less* than a meter?

3. the height of your chair

   more   less   than 1 meter

4. the height of a door

   more   less   than 1 meter

Is it *more* than or *less* than a kilometer?

5. the distance that an airplane flies

   more   less   than a kilometer

6. the distance from your chair to the school office

   more   less   than a kilometer

Complete each sentence. Write *cm, m,* or *km.*

7. Hannah's jump rope is about 1 _____ long.

8. The distance around the playground is about 2 _____ .

9. A baseball bat is about 85 _____ long.

Solve.

10. Jared can run 1 kilometer in about 8 minutes. How long will it take him to run 7 kilometers?

   _____

11. In the softball toss, Abby threw distances of 28 meters and 37 meters. What is the combined distance?

   _____

HEALTH CONNECTION

12. Here are Olympic running events. Ring the events whose distances are 1 kilometer or greater.

   100-meter run   200-meter run   400-meter run   800-meter run

   1,000-meter run   1,500-meter run   10,000 meter run

Use with text pages 332–333.

Name _____

Capacity
Milliliter and Liter

Choose the unit you would use to measure each.
Write *milliliter* or *liter.*

1. water in a thimble

2. milk in a cup

3. orange juice in a jug

_____   _____   _____

Ring the better estimate.

4.

2 mL or 2 L

5.

250 mL or 250 L

6.

6 mL or 6 L

Mixed Applications

7. Henry filled his cat's 500-mL water dish this morning. Now the dish has 175 mL of water. How much did the cat drink?

_____

8. A small can of juice contains 650 mL. The large can holds 1,000 mL. How many more mL does the large can of juice hold?

_____

9. Yoko combines 875 mL of white paint and 250 mL of red paint. Does Yoko make *more* than or *less* than 1,000 mL of pink paint?

_____

10. A 25-L pot of soup is divided equally into 5 smaller containers for storage. How much soup does each container hold?

_____

WRITER'S CORNER

11. Make a list of foods, liquids and household items that may come in containers holding about 1 liter.

Food _____

Liquids _____

Household Items _____

Use with text pages 334–335.

Exploring Weight
Gram and Kilogram

Which unit of measure would you use to weigh each
item? Write *gram* or *kilogram.*

1. an envelope

2. a crayon

3. a desk

_____   _____   _____

Complete each sentence. Write *grams* or *kilograms.*

4. Vic's dog weighs about 10 _____ .

5. The dog's bone weighs about 65 _____ .

Use the graph for Exercises 6–8.

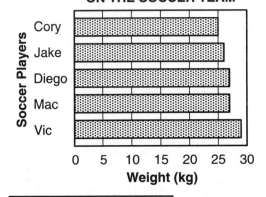

**WEIGHT OF SOME PLAYERS
ON THE SOCCER TEAM**

6. Which student weighs the
   most?

   _____

7. Which students are the same
   weight?

   _____

8. Write Cory's and Jake's weight.

   _____

MIXED REVIEW

Find the sum or difference.

1. $4.25 + 1.79	2. $18.97 + 10.75	3. 600 − 236	4. 4,290 +2,175	5. 8,125 − 1,023

Ring the figures that are congruent to the first one.

6.

Exploring Celsius Temperature

Ring the more reasonable temperature.

1. hot cereal

   – 30°C or 90°C

2. ice cube

   20°C or 0°C

3. picnic weather

   20°C or 80°C

4. room temperature

   20°C or 70°C

5. swimming weather

   – 30°C or 30°C

6. frozen yogurt

   20°C or – 5°C

Write each temperature.

7.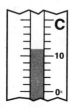

_____

8.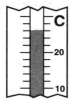

_____

9.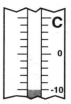

_____

Solve.

10. Edgar must increase the oven temperature by 15°C every half hour for a science project. He started at 90°C at 1:30 P.M. What should the temperature be at 3:00 P.M.?

_____

11. Gretel bakes bread. Bread needs to bake at 150°C. Gretel's oven does not work well. It cooks 20°C hotter than it should. At what temperature should Gretel set her oven?

_____

LOGICAL REASONING

12. In Newton the temperature is 11°C. In Shannon the temperature is 20°C higher than in Newton. In Las Palos it is 10°C colder than in Shannon. In Richmond, it is 5°C warmer than in Las Palos. List the cities from lowest to highest temperatures.

_____

Problem Solving
Use a Bar Graph

Use the bar graph for Exercises 1–2.

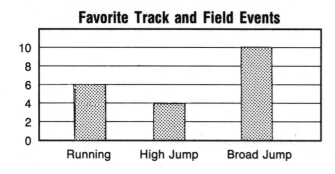

Favorite Track and Field Events

1. Which event is the favorite?

   _____

2. How many more students voted for the broad jump than for the high jump?

   _____

Mixed Applications

STRATEGIES	• Act It Out • Draw a Picture • Write a Number Sentence • Work Backward

Choose a strategy and solve.

3. Della's soccer ball was reduced from $9.50 to $7.97. How much money did Della save by buying the ball at the reduced price?

   _____

4. Juanita measures her new tennis racket. The stringed head is 9 inches. The handle is 11 inches. What is the racket's length?

   _____

5. A square field measures 6 yards on each side. What is the perimeter of the field?

   _____

6. On Saturday, Tad jogged from 1:55 until 2:40. For how long did Tad jog?

   _____

VISUAL THINKING

7. Mr. Ming may swim the perimeter of Pool A or Pool B. In which pool must he swim farther? How much farther?

   _____

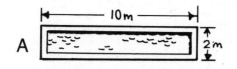

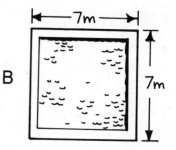

Exploring Fractions

Write the fraction for the part that is shaded.
Then say the fraction.

1. ☐ shaded parts
_____
☐ parts in all

2. ☐ shaded parts
_____
☐ parts in all

3. 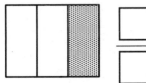 ☐
_____
☐

4. 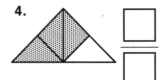 ☐
_____
☐

5. ☐
_____
☐

Write the fraction for the part that is shaded.

6. 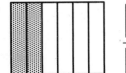 ☐
_____
☐

7. ☐
_____
☐

8. ☐
_____
☐

Write the fraction for each word name.

9. one third ☐
_____
☐

10. two fifths ☐
_____
☐

11. four sixths ☐
_____
☐

EVERYDAY MATH CONNECTION

Many foods must be divided into fractional parts in
order for people to share them. Shade one fourth of
each food item to show one serving out of four.

12.

13.

14.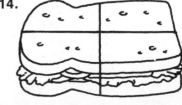

Use with text pages 350–351.

Name _____

Name _____

Exploring Part of a Group

12.2

USE WHAT YOU KNOW

Write the fraction for the part that is shaded. Tell if each shows *part of a whole* or *part of a group*.

1.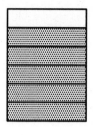

_____

2.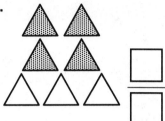

_____

3.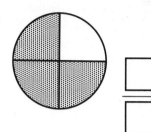

_____

4.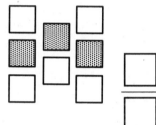

_____

5.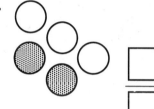

_____

6.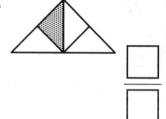

_____

Write the fraction that names the part of the group described.

7. boxes with bows

8. Polka dot ribbons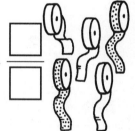

SCIENCE CONNECTION

Evelyn planted flower seeds all around her garden.

Shade the flowers that bloomed in Evelyn's garden.

9.

Three sevenths are red.
Four sevenths are blue.

10.

Five eighths are orange.
Three eighths are yellow.

Use with text pages 352–353.

P 121

Finding Part of a Group

Manipulatives

Use counters to find $\frac{1}{3}$ of each group. Write the
number sentence.

1.

_____

2.

_____

3.

_____

Use counters to find $\frac{1}{5}$ of each group. Write the
number sentence.

4.

_____

5.

_____

6.

_____

Mixed Applications

7. Sam bought 12 apples. He used $\frac{1}{4}$ of them to make an apple pie. How many apples did Sam use?

_____

8. Ruth had \$4. She spent $\frac{1}{2}$ of her money on lunch. How much money did she have left?

_____

VISUAL THINKING

9.

How many circles are there? _____

How many circles are in $\frac{1}{3}$ of the group?

_____

To find the circles in $\frac{2}{3}$ of the group, you count the number in 2 out of 3, or $\frac{2}{3}$ of the rows. How many circles are in $\frac{2}{3}$ of the group?

_____

Use with text pages 354–355.

Name _____

Exploring Equivalent Fractions

Write *true* or *false*.

1.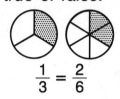

$$\frac{1}{3} = \frac{2}{6}$$

_____

2.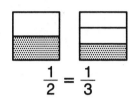

$$\frac{1}{2} = \frac{1}{3}$$

_____

3.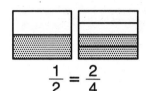

$$\frac{1}{2} = \frac{2}{4}$$

_____

4.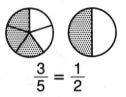

$$\frac{3}{5} = \frac{1}{2}$$

_____

5.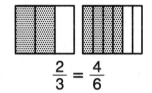

$$\frac{2}{3} = \frac{4}{6}$$

_____

6.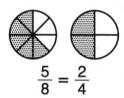

$$\frac{5}{8} = \frac{2}{4}$$

_____

Name the equivalent fraction.

7.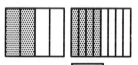

$$\frac{2}{4} = \frac{\square}{8}$$

8.

$$\frac{5}{10} = \frac{\square}{2}$$

9.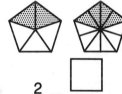

$$\frac{2}{5} = \frac{\square}{10}$$

10.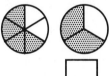

$$\frac{4}{6} = \frac{\square}{3}$$

11.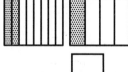

$$\frac{2}{8} = \frac{\square}{4}$$

12.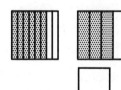

$$\frac{6}{8} = \frac{\square}{4}$$

MIXED REVIEW

Find the product or quotient.

1. $\begin{array}{r} 5 \\ \times 3 \\ \hline \end{array}$
2. $\begin{array}{r} 8 \\ \times 5 \\ \hline \end{array}$
3. $\begin{array}{r} 7 \\ \times 7 \\ \hline \end{array}$
4. $\begin{array}{r} 4 \\ \times 9 \\ \hline \end{array}$
5. $\begin{array}{r} 9 \\ \times 6 \\ \hline \end{array}$
6. $\begin{array}{r} 0 \\ \times 2 \\ \hline \end{array}$

7. $4\overline{)32}$
8. $5\overline{)45}$
9. $4\overline{)28}$
10. $8\overline{)48}$
11. $6\overline{)36}$

Use with text pages 356–357.

Name _____

Exploring Comparing Fractions

Compare. Write < or > in each $\bigcirc$.

1.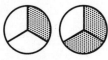

$\frac{1}{3} \bigcirc \frac{2}{3}$

2.

$\frac{3}{4} \bigcirc \frac{2}{4}$

3.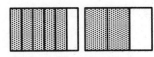

$\frac{5}{6} \bigcirc \frac{2}{3}$

Compare. Write <, >, or = in each $\bigcirc$.

4.

$\frac{3}{5} \bigcirc \frac{4}{5}$

5.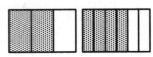

$\frac{2}{3} \bigcirc \frac{4}{6}$

6.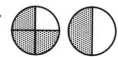

$\frac{3}{4} \bigcirc \frac{1}{2}$

7.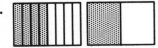

$\frac{4}{8} \bigcirc \frac{1}{2}$

8.

$\frac{3}{5} \bigcirc \frac{3}{8}$

9.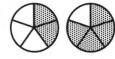

$\frac{2}{5} \bigcirc \frac{4}{5}$

Solve.

10. Quint has finished $\frac{2}{5}$ of his math homework. Greta has completed $\frac{2}{3}$ of the same homework. Who has completed more?

_____

11. A bowl of muffin batter contains $\frac{1}{3}$-cup of oil and $\frac{2}{3}$-cup of milk. Do the muffins have more *milk* or more *oil*?

_____

WRITER'S CORNER ————————————————

12. Two pizzas are equal in size. One is cut into 6 equal pieces. The other is cut into 8 equal pieces. Which pizza has larger pieces? Explain your answer.

_____

_____

Use with text pages 358–359.

Name _____

Mixed Numbers

Draw a picture to show the mixed number.

1. Draw 4 rectangles.
   Color $3\frac{1}{5}$ rectangles yellow.

2. Draw 2 rectangles.
   Color $1\frac{4}{4}$ rectangles green.

Use the ruler. Choose the best answer. Ring **a, b,** or **c.**

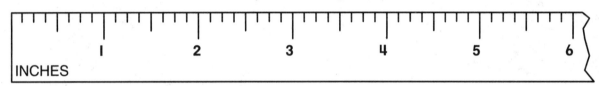

3. Two and one-eighth inches is
   closest to _____ inches.

   a. 1   b. 2   c. 3

4. One and seven-eighths is
   closest to _____ inches.

   a. 1   b. 2   c. 3

Complete the pattern.

5. $\frac{1}{4}$, $\frac{2}{4}$, $\frac{3}{4}$, 1, $1\frac{1}{4}$, $1\frac{2}{4}$, _____, _____, _____

Mixed Applications

6. Marta ate $\frac{1}{6}$ of a pie.
   Yoki ate $\frac{2}{6}$ of a pie.
   Who ate more?

   _____

7. At closing time Mr. Pizza still
   had $2\frac{7}{8}$ unsold pizzas. Is this
   closer to *2 pizzas* or *3 pizzas*?

   _____

VISUAL THINKING
---

8. Write the mixed number that names the shaded
   part. Order the numbers from least to greatest.

   _____

 _____   _____   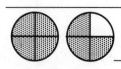 _____

Exploring Probability

Look at the spinner. Write the correct answer.

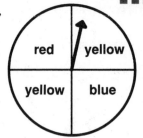

1. What are the chances that the pointer will stop on red?

_____

2. What are the chances that the pointer will stop on yellow?

_____

3. On which color is the spinner most likely to stop? Why?

_____

What are the chances of picking an orange? Ring **a** or **b**.

4.

   a. 1 out of 4

   b. 1 out of 5

5.

   a. 1 out of 4

   b. 2 out of 4

Suppose you drop a cube several times on each gameboard.

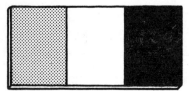  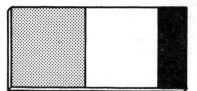

6. On which board is a cube most likely to land on white? Why?

_____

7. On which board is a cube least likely to land on black? Why?

_____

8. Which board is a fair board? Why? _____

VISUAL THINKING

9. Color the circles in the bag. Make the chances of drawing

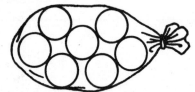

red: 1 out of 7.   yellow: 3 out of 7.
green: 1 out of 7.   blue: 2 out of 7.

Problem-Solving Strategy
Draw a Picture

Solve. Use the strategy *draw a picture.*

1. At Harry's Uniform Shop, $\frac{1}{2}$ of the uniforms are red, $\frac{2}{5}$ are blue, and $\frac{3}{10}$ are gold. Of which color uniform does Harry have the most?

2. Harry sells 15 gold uniforms. He has matching helmets for only $\frac{1}{3}$ of the uniforms. How many helmets is he missing?

_____

_____

Mixed Applications ⟩ **STRATEGIES** • Guess and Check • Draw a Picture • Act It Out • Find a Pattern

Choose a strategy and solve.

3. A carousel ride costs $4 for adults and $3 for children. Mr. Sanchez pays $23 for 7 people. For how many adults does he pay? How many children?

4. A gameboard has 27 squares. Each square is red or blue. The number of red squares is two times the number of blue squares. How many squares of each color are there?

_____

_____

WRITER'S CORNER

5. Write a problem about this picture.

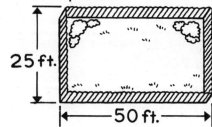

25 ft.

50 ft.

_____

_____

_____

Name _____

Name _____

Decimals
Tenths

Write the decimal for the part that is shaded.

1.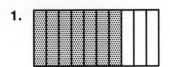

2.

3.

_____   _____   _____

Write each fraction as a decimal.

4. $\frac{2}{10}$ _____   5. $\frac{5}{10}$ _____   6. $\frac{9}{10}$ _____   7. $\frac{3}{10}$ _____

Write each decimal as a fraction.

8. 0.4 ▢/▢   9. 0.8 ▢/▢   10. 0.1 ▢/▢   11. 0.6 ▢/▢

Mixed Applications

Write each answer as a fraction and as a decimal.

12. In one tennis match, Chris won 6 out of 10 games. What part of the games did Chris win?

_____

13. Jaime served the ball 10 times. He scored a pont on his serve 3 of those times. On what part of his serves did Jaime score a point?

_____

NUMBER SENSE

14. Write each as a decimal. Then order the decimals in each set from least to greatest. Write *1, 2, 3,* or *4* in each box.

$\frac{3}{10}$ _____ ▢ $\frac{2}{10}$ _____ ▢

seven tenths _____ ▢   five tenths _____ ▢

Name _____

Decimals
Hundredths

Write the decimal that tells what part is shaded.

1. 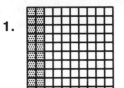 _____

2. 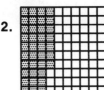 _____

Write each fraction as a decimal

3. $\frac{83}{100}$ _____

4. $\frac{48}{100}$ _____

5. $\frac{9}{100}$ _____

Write each decimal as an amount of money.

6. forty-five hundredths _____

7. sixty-two hundredths _____

Use the place-value chart for Exercises 8–9.

8. In 0.56, what digit is in the hundredths place? _____

9. In 0.34, in what place is the digit 0? _____

Ones	.	Tenths	Hundredths
0	.	5	6
0	.	3	4

Mixed Applications

10. Marcy spent 60 cents on a pen and 10 cents on an eraser. Write the amount that Marcy spent as a decimal and as a dollar amount.

_____

11. Mr. Quest had 100 squiggle pencils to sell. He sold 30 of them in one hour. Write the number of pencils sold as a fraction and a decimal.

_____

LOGICAL REASONING ─────────────────────

12. How would a place-value chart show decimal parts of a dollar? Complete the chart headings.

$		Dimes	
1	•	0	0

Name _____

Decimals Greater Than I

Write a decimal for the part that is shaded.

1.

2.

3.

_____   _____   _____

Write each mixed number as a decimal.

4. $6\frac{7}{10}$ _____

5. $12\frac{72}{100}$ _____

6. $27\frac{4}{100}$ _____

Write each decimal as a mixed number.

7. 4.3 _____

8. 9.03 _____

9. 67.29 _____

Write each decimal in words.

10. 4.7 _____

11. 8.92 _____

Mixed Applications

12. Fred bought a toy bat and ball for $3.17. The bat cost $1.98. How much was the ball?

_____

13. Susan and Jeff each had a dollar. Susan spent $\frac{1}{2}$ of her dollar. Jeff spent $\frac{3}{4}$ of his dollar. Who spent more?

_____

WRITER'S CORNER

14. Explain how you can tell that 0.3 is equal to 0.30.

_____

_____

_____

Decimals
Adding and Subtracting

Find the sum or difference.

1. 3.4 +2.5	2. 2.6 +3.7	3. 2.5 +5.5	4. 3.19 +4.56	5. 4.10 +2.88
6. 5.9 −2.5	7. 9.1 −1.9	8. 8.1 −6.3	9. 8.15 −5.90	10. 6.00 −4.50
11. 1.9 +7.9	12. 7.2 −4.5	13. 3.72 +5.25	14. 9.35 −3.28	15. 7.88 +1.45

Mixed Applications

16. The daytime temperature one day was 72.8 degrees. The temperature dropped 23.5 degrees by nightfall. What was the temperature then?

_____

17. Sam ran the 10-kilometer race in 53.25 minutes. It took Ed 49.80 minutes to run the same race.

a. Who ran faster? _____

b. How much faster? _____

MIXED REVIEW

Write the temperature shown in degrees Celsius.

1.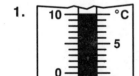

_____

2.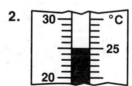

_____

3.

_____

Write the missing number.

4. $9 \times$ _____ $= 63$ 5. $4 \times$ _____ $= 32$ 6. $81 \div$ _____ $= 9$

7. $48 \div$ _____ $= 8$ 8. $16 \div$ _____ $= 4$ 9. $5 \times$ _____ $= 45$

Problem Solving
Multistep Problems

1. There were 4 cans of tennis balls with 3 balls in each can. Luis and Jane lost 7 balls. How many are left?

   _____

2. Mona played tennis with Jill from 9:30 until 10:15. She played with Rita from 2:45 until 3:35. For how long did Mona play tennis?

   _____

Mixed Applications ⟩	**STRATEGIES**	• Write a Number Sentence • Guess and Check • Work Backward •Draw a Picture

Choose a strategy and solve.

3. There are 12 muffins on a baker's rack. Of these, $\frac{1}{3}$ are blueberry muffins and $\frac{1}{2}$ are bran muffins. How many blueberry muffins are there? How many bran muffins?

   _____

4. Sean bought a basketball for $12.88 and a football for $9.75. How much more did the basketball cost?

   _____

VISUAL THINKING

Bag A    Bag B

5. From which bag are you more likely to draw a shaded marble? Explain by telling the chances of getting a shaded marble in each case.

   _____

   _____

Exploring Multiplying Tens and Hundreds

Manipulatives

Copy and complete. Use mental math or place-value materials to help you.

1. $3 \times 7 = 3 \times 7$ _____ = _____ ones = 21

   $3 \times 70 = 3 \times 7$ _____ = _____ tens = _____

   $3 \times 700 = 3 \times 7$ _____ = _____ hundreds = _____

2. Since $3 \times 3 = 9$, $3 \times 30 =$ _____ , and $3 \times 300 =$ _____

3. Since $5 \times 7 = 35$, $5 \times 70 =$ _____ , and $5 \times 700 =$ _____

4. $4 \times 3 =$ _____   5. $3 \times 9 =$ _____   6. $6 \times 5 =$ _____

   $4 \times 30 =$ _____ $3 \times 90 =$ _____ $6 \times 50 =$ _____

   $4 \times 300 =$ _____ $3 \times 900 =$ _____ $6 \times 500 =$ _____

7. 50	8. 400	9. 30	10. 80	11. 900
× 4	× 9	× 5	× 7	× 6

VISUAL THINKING

Write multiplication number sentences to describe the pictures.

12.

13.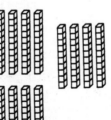

14.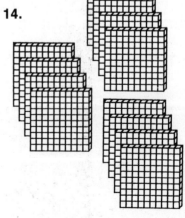

_____   _____

Exploring Multiplying Two-Digit Numbers

Manipulatives

Find the total. Use place-value materials to help you.

1. 4 groups of 15 = _____

2. 3 groups of 24 = _____

3. 3 groups of 16 = _____

4. 2 groups of 37 = _____

Find the product. Use place-value materials to help you.

5. $3 \times 13 =$ ____

6. $5 \times 15 =$ ____

7. $2 \times 28 =$ ____

8. $8 \times 12 =$ ____

9. $4 \times 16 =$ ____

10. $2 \times 43 =$ ____

11. $3 \times 25 =$ ____

12. $4 \times 18 =$ ____

13. two times twenty-nine = _____

14. four times thirty-one = _____

15. The students in each of 4 classes at Andian School recycled 27 foam lunch trays on Monday. How many trays did they recycle on Monday?

_____

16. Foam lunch trays cost George's school about 2¢ each. How much money does the school save by recycling 27 lunch trays?

_____

CONSUMER CONNECTION

Recycling centers around the country pay 5¢ for every aluminum can or bottle returned to be recycled. Find the total amount earned by each student.

17.

18.

19.

_____   _____   _____

Name _____

Multiplying Two-Digit Numbers

Manipulatives

Find the product. Use place-value materials to help you.

1. 27
   × 2

2. 18
   × 3

3. 42
   × 2

4. 38
   × 2

5. 17
   × 5

6. 19
   × 4

7. 23
   × 4

8. 34
   × 2

9. 16
   × 5

10. 22
    × 4

11. 25
    × 3

12. 18
    × 2

13. 18 × 4 = _____

14. 28 × 3 = _____

15. 13 × 5 = _____

16. 4 × 13 = _____

17. 3 × 24 = _____

18. 5 × 16 = _____

Mixed Applications

19. A senator receives 2 letters a day from students who support the Clean Air Bill. How many letters does the senator receive in a 31-day month?

_____

20. Ms. Dey's class checked the temperature 3 times a day. How many readings would they collect at the end of a 4-week period?

_____

SOCIAL STUDIES CONNECTION

In 1989, President Bush proposed a Clean Air program. Cars would run on natural gas or other, less poisonous gases. The cost of the program for the automobile industry would be up to $19 billion a year.

What might the Clean Air program cost in:

21. 2 years? _____

22. 3 years? _____

23. 4 years? _____

24. 5 years? _____

Regrouping Ones and Tens

Manipulatives

Find the product. Use place-value materials to help you.

1. 63 × 2	2. 42 × 3	3. 83 × 2	4. 36 × 4	5. 71 × 5	6. 52 × 4

7. 12 × 8	8. 34 × 5	9. 31 × 6	10. 33 × 4	11. 42 × 4	12. 28 × 6

13. $4 \times 45 =$ _____   14. $3 \times 39 =$ _____   15. $3 \times 72 =$ _____

Mixed Applications

16. Teri works at a recycling center. She earns $8 an hour. How much money does she earn in a 35-hour work week?

_____

17. The center received 5,102 cans in March and 3,574 cans in April. How many more cans did the center receive in March than in April?

_____

MIXED REVIEW

Solve.

1.

$\frac{1}{4}$ of 12 = _____

2.

$\frac{1}{3}$ of 15 = _____

3. 4.2 +5.8	4. 9.7 −1.9	5. 3.45 +2.73	6. 4.15 −0.97	7. 8.95 −2.71

Multiplying Three-Digit Numbers

Find the product.

1. 103
× 8

2. 215
× 3

3. 141
× 7

4. 274
× 2

5. 225
× 4

6. 150
× 5

7. 342
× 5

8. 468
× 2

9. 591
× 4

10. 412
× 8

11. 154
× 6

12. 807
× 3

13. 360
× 3

14. 903
× 5

15. 223
× 4

16. 649
× 2

17. 164
× 5

18. 650
× 7

19. 6 × 145 = _____

20. 7 × 24 = _____

21. 5 × 112 = _____

Mixed Applications

22. There are 112 acres in each section of a wildlife preserve. How many acres are in 7 sections?

_____

23. Each ticket to a national park costs $5.75. How much money do 4 tickets cost?

_____

NUMBER SENSE

24. Write a multiplication problem in which you do not need to regroup. How did you choose your numbers? Explain.

× _____

_____
_____
_____
_____

Estimating Products

Estimate by rounding. Tell whether the estimate is *greater* than or *less* than your exact answer.

1. 37 × 4	2. 91 × 3	3. 53 × 5	4. 780 × 6	5. 305 × 8	6. 419 × 7

_____   _____   _____   _____   _____   _____

Estimate using front digits. Tell whether the estimate is *greater* than or *less* than your exact answer.

7. 83 × 3	8. 49 × 2	9. 215 × 4	10. 573 × 7	11. 188 × 9	12. 720 × 6

_____   _____   _____   _____   _____   _____

Mixed Applications

13. A recycling center can process 930 pounds of paper each day. Estimate how many pounds can be processed in 5 days.

_____

14. A large barrel holds 72 pounds of used paper. About how many pounds of paper would 6 barrels hold?

_____

WRITER'S CORNER

15. Look at Exercises 1–6. When is your estimate greater than the actual product? When is it less than the actual product? Write a sentence to explain.

_____

_____

_____

_____

                                    Use with text pages 396–397.

Problem-Solving Strategy
Use Estimation

Solve. Use estimation.

1. A watering can costs $6.35. A shovel costs $4.55. A spade costs $3.15. Estimate the total cost for all three items.

_____

2. Tickets for a ride cost $4.05 for adults and $2.15 for children. Estimate how much two adults and three children would pay.

_____

| Mixed Applications ⟩ | STRATEGIES | •Write a Number Sentence • Act It Out • Work Backward • Draw a Picture |

Choose a strategy and solve.

3. Scouts are planting maple trees at the bottom of Climb Hill. They plant oak trees nearer the top of the hill than the spruce trees. Pine trees are planted at the top of the hill. In what order are the trees planted from top to bottom?

_____

4. Hip Heating promises a savings of $15.50 on your monthly electric bill if you set your thermostat at 62 degrees each night. The Wu family's bill was $89.35 with Hip. What would they have paid if they had not used Hip?

_____

SCIENCE CONNECTION

At the San Diego Zoo, animals eat about 225 pounds of barley, 79 pounds of seeds, and 55 bushels of apples in one week.

About how much food does the San Diego Zoo need for each time period? Estimate by rounding.

	Time Period	Barley (pounds)	Seeds (pounds)	Apples (bushels)
5.	2 weeks			
6.	4 weeks			
7.	8 weeks			

Exploring Division Patterns

Show the quotients on the place-value chart.

Place-Value Chart

Hundreds	Tens	Ones

1. 8 ÷ 4

    80 ÷ 4

    800 ÷ 4

Place-Value Chart

Hundreds	Tens	Ones

2. 20 ÷ 5

    200 ÷ 5

    2,000 ÷ 5

Use mental math to find the quotient.

3. 4)‾80‾

4. 2)‾60‾

5. 6)‾360‾

6. 5)‾250‾

7. 7)‾350‾

8. There were 120 people at the rally. They arrived in 3 buses. Each bus held the same number of people. How many people were on each bus?

_____

9. Carlos mailed 320 fliers. He mailed the same number of fliers on each of 4 days. How many fliers did Carlos mail each day?

_____

VISUAL THINKING

How much money each person will receive if each group of ten-dollar bills is divided evenly among 4 people. Write a number sentence.

10.

11.

12.

_____   _____   _____

_____   _____   _____

Exploring Quotients with Remainders

Manipulatives

Use your counters. Find the quotient.

1. 3)28 2. 4)32 3. 5)27 4. 8)35 5. 2)17

6. 9)83 7. 8)47 8. 6)37 9. 7)49 10. 4)39

11. 8)42 12. 4)19 13. 9)60 14. 7)58 15. 5)45

16. 7)25 17. 5)29 18. 9)29 19. 8)43 20. 9)37

MIXED REVIEW

Identify each figure.

1.    2.    3.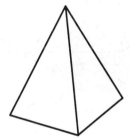

_____   _____   _____

Compare the numbers. Write <, >, or = in the ◯.

4. 78 ◯ 87   5. 193 ◯ 193   6. 5,222 ◯ 5,227

7. 7,031 ◯ 7,310   8. 1,140 ◯ 920   9. 35,190 ◯ 25,198

Find the sum.

10. $1.15
    + 1.15

11. $5.09
    + 3.26

12. $2.67
    + 1.93

13. $3.22
    + 6.06

14. $8.45
    + 4.81

Exploring Two-Digit Quotients with Remainders

Find the quotient. Use your place-value materials.
Then check each answer by using multiplication.

1. 47 ÷ 3   3)47

Check:

2. 35 ÷ 2   2)35

Check:

3. 53 ÷ 4   4)53

Check:

4. 55 ÷ 2   2)55

Check:

5. 58 ÷ 3   3)58

Check:

6. 69 ÷ 5   5)69

Check:

7. 29 ÷ 2   2)29

Check:

8. 52 ÷ 3   3)52

Check:

9. 75 ÷ 4   4)75

Check:

VISUAL THINKING

10. Write a division problem and its multiplication
check for this example.

Use with text pages 406–407.

Problem Solving
Choose a Strategy

→ Mixed Applications

STRATEGIES

• Find a Pattern • Guess and Check
• Work Backward • Draw a Picture
• Write a Number Sentence

Choose a strategy and solve.

1. Tamara finished her homework at 4:15. She had been working for 45 minutes. What time did she begin her homework?

_____

2. Mrs. Edgar reviewed the math homework. Tamara got $\frac{1}{5}$ of the 20 math exercises wrong. How many were correct?

_____

3. Ramón and Stan were playing a game. Ramón said 10, Stan said 15. Ramón said 25, Stan said 30. Ramón said 50, Stan said 55. What did Stan say when Ramón said 85?

_____

4. Jules and Jordan collected 24 cans for the recycling drive. Jules collected twice as many as Jordan. How many cans did Jules and Jordan collect?

_____

WRITER'S CORNER

5. Write a problem using information from the bar graph. Exchange with a partner. Solve.

_____

_____

_____

_____

_____

_____

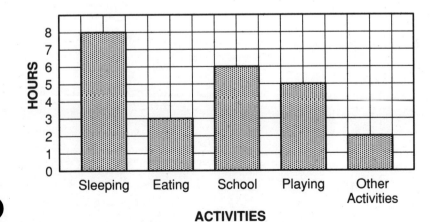